Bosses are hired ...
LEADERSHIP
IS EARNED

Experiences. Lessons.
Decisions. Life.

PRAISE FOR
BOSSES ARE HIRED ...
LEADERSHIP
IS EARNED

"I've long admired Carson as a leader, always engaging with his staff, learning from others, courageous in ensuring development and progress for the people he leads (as well as sound and considered contribution to the overall business agenda). I'm delighted he has written this book, and I love the storytelling approach, which makes the book easy to read and makes the key learnings easy to remember. This is a must-have book!"

Anton Herbig
Retired Divisional Vice President of Operations, Abbott Laboratories

"This is not another boring 'how to be a good boss' book. The stories Carson shares are real, insightful, and full of lessons you can use to grow in your career. I've personally seen Carson lead using these life lessons that he is sharing. This is a book you'll go back to multiple times, to help you earn good leadership skills."

Norma Noble
Senior Manager, R&D Project Management, ThermoFisher Scientific

"Bosses Are Hired ... Leadership Is Earned is a heartfelt reminder that great leaders are shaped as much by those they've had the privilege to lead as those they've been led by. Carson encourages us to take inventory of the experiences and people who have helped us throughout our careers, and reminds us of our obligation to pass that gift on to others!"

Chris Herrick
Chief Human Resources Officer. OMEGA Engineering

"Carson Sublett has not only hit on core principles of great leadership in this book, but has found the 'secret sauce' to sharing them: stories! Stories connect with people in ways that mere facts and information can't. They help us grasp truths, internalize them, and put them into practice. The combination of solid leadership principles and great life stories makes this one leadership book I don't want to put down."

Senior Pastor Phillip Lee
Cedar Creek Church

"As an Army leader of three decades who has experienced the combat crucible of leadership, I found this to be a fantastic book for anyone who leads the very lifeblood of business: its people!"

Colonel Rob Campbell
United States Army, Retired, Author of *It's Personal, Not Personnel: Leadership Lessons for the Battlefield and the Boardroom*

"Bosses Are Hired ... Leadership Is Earned provides insights into Carson's mindset of inclusion and teaches readers how to build teams to overcome Herculean challenges and to overachieve targets. If you're an aspiring manager, a new leader just starting out, or even a well-tenured executive, you're bound to find Carson's lessons on leadership of significant value to you."

Alex Cooke
Managing Director and Owner, Phase 3 Search, LLC

"I got to know Carson as an excellent leader and great human being during my time as President and CEO of DSM Pharmaceutical Products. I found the stories shared by Carson in his book to be, at the same time, entertaining and insightful. I appreciate his openness to share lessons he's learned and principles I've seen him put into practice."

Alexander R. Wessels
Chief Executive Officer, Archroma (Switzerland)

"Stories are perhaps the best way to engage an audience — whether that audience is one person or a packed auditorium. Carson uses the art of storytelling to provide insights into what encounters, mentors, and lessons learned along the way can forge a person into an effective leader. Each chapter of this book is a snapshot of those experiences, providing insights into personal growth that we would be wise to consider as we make our own journeys from 'boss' to 'leader.' It is said that a smart man learns from his mistakes but a truly wise man learns from the experiences (good and bad) of others. Carson provides us with that valuable opportunity in this book."

David B. Amerine
Retired Nuclear Industry Executive, Author of *Push It to Move It: Lessons Learned from a Career in Nuclear Project Management*

"Through interesting stories from his career and profiles of really great people he's met along the way, Carson's approach to showing us how to earn our leadership stripes is a really fresh take on the subject matter of leadership. He teaches us that some of the greatest leadership lessons don't actually come from leaders themselves but rather from those who have been led. If I had a company, I would use Carson's book to teach our next generation of leaders."

Chris Clews
Keynote Speaker and Author of the Book Series
What '80s Pop Culture Teaches Us About Today's Workplace

"As a young leader in local government, I have experienced the importance of earning respect. I look forward to sharing Carson's lessons of humility, integrity, and success with colleagues and carrying them throughout my career."

Spencer Wetmore
City Administrator, City of Folly Beach

"*Bosses Are Hired ... Leadership Is Earned* is a must-read for any developing or aspiring leaders who are starting their careers in business, the military, or still at university. The author Carson Sublett knows what he is talking about. I had an opportunity to see him in action as an outstanding leader for over 20 years at GlaxoSmithKline, first as an HR director and then as a manufacturing site VP leading one of our consumer manufacturing facilities. Carson's story about his first job right out of college as a shift supervisor at a textile mill is a terrific look at a wet-behind-the-ears young man who learns the ropes from an old hand working for him. All of the vignettes are equally powerful. Enjoy and see how leadership is earned."

Dan Phelan
Former Senior Vice-President, Human Resources, and Chief of Staff

"Carson's book confirms what I learned first-hand during our years working together. He is among that rare breed of business leaders with the ability to tell stories that inspire and instruct, told with humanity and humility. *Bosses Are Hired ... Leadership Is Earned* is an essential book by an extraordinary leader."

Darren A. Singer
Group Vice President, higi; Former Colleague of Carson's While VP/Site Director at GSK Consumer Healthcare

"A great book for both leaders and employees! The personal stories are entertaining and relatable, and the lessons learned are thought provoking. A fantastic read for anyone looking for professional and personal growth. Excellent work, Carson!"

Syd Kitson
CEO of the Kitson Group

"I have been lucky enough to work with and for Carson for a good portion of the past 10 years. He has been the single biggest influence on my career and in particular the leadership component of it. Put simply, he showed me how to be a true grown-up in the workplace. By that I mean how to lead by example, be accountable, and be respectful, and how good people flourish under good leaders and can transform a business."

Chris Holt
Site Head and GM of AGC Biologics

"I have always lived by the thought that the boss has the title, while a leader has the people. Carson's stories and 'lessons learned' are consistent with that belief. I greatly appreciate Carson sharing his life stories openly so we can all become better leaders."

Bill Rich
Consultant, Retired VP of Device Technology for Amgen

"Carson captures — in a simple, straightforward way — gems of leadership truths distilled from the complexities and subtleties of a highly successful business career. In our world screaming for more and better leadership in business, government, religious and other organizations, he outlines important insights and applications for those actively bettering their own leadership journey."

Laura L. Parks, PhD
Community Volunteer, Retired Biopharmaceutical Industry Executive

"Carson is a great leader and in his superb book, *Bosses Are Hired ... Leadership Is Earned*, he shares stories that give insight, inspiration and practical tips on putting his knowledge into practice. It's a must-read."

Giles Long, MBE
Triple Paralympic Gold Medalist, and CEO of Lexicon Decoder

"If you're a connoisseur of leadership, Carson's book is a must-read. Through his smooth-flowing stories and lessons learned, Carson has captured the essence of the 'how' people earn the recognition of being a real leader. I wholeheartedly identify with Carson's book title, *Bosses Are Hired ... Leadership Is Earned*, and couldn't agree more. Great job, Carson!"

Robert "Bo" Brabo
VP of Human Resources, The National Spine & Pain Centers, and Author of *From the Battlefield to the White House to the Board Room: Leading Organizations to Values-Based Results*

Bosses are hired ...

LEADERSHIP
IS EARNED

Experiences. Lessons.
Decisions. Life.

CARSON SUBLETT

 SILVER TREE
PUBLISHING

Bosses Are Hired ... Leadership Is Earned:
Experiences. Lessons. Decisions. Life.

Copyright 2019 by Carson Sublett

Published by Silver Tree Publishing, a division of
Silver Tree Communications, LLC (Kenosha, WI).
www.SilverTreePublishing.com

Editing by:
Kate Colbert

Cover design and typesetting by:
Courtney Hudson

First edition, November 2019

ISBN: 978-1-948238-18-2

Library of Congress Control Number: 2019911967

Created in the United States of America

TABLE OF CONTENTS

FOREWORD

by Tim Doke

As you read through the stories in Carson Sublett's authoritative guide to what he calls "earned leadership," you ultimately will come upon this profound statement:

"While there are times when people succeed with motivations that would not hold up in the court of public scrutiny, leaders who never waiver from the right foundations ultimately will succeed."

During my 43-year career as an executive with some of the world's largest companies and biggest brands (where I most frequently reported directly to the CEO), I encountered many different leadership styles. And, coincidentally, the common success factor was never wavering from the right foundation. Great leaders are not defined by their position, title or educational pedigree. They are characterized instead by their core beliefs and practices that motivate their behaviors and decisions.

Great leaders are not defined by their position, title or educational pedigree. They are characterized instead by their core beliefs and practices that motivate their behaviors and decisions.

Although I never ran large manufacturing facilities or pharmaceutical operations, as Carson has, I found the stories included here in his book to be directly parallel to my own career in communications, reputation management and marketing. For me, this universal application of Carson's insights underscored that basic leadership principles are indifferent to the type of business or organization in which you work. And, I think you'll find it's the very same with the lessons learned articulated in this book.

Storytelling is a powerful device, the potency of which I was fortunate to learn at age 20 while driving several hours over a couple of days with the late Alex Haley, two years before he wrote the blockbuster novel *Roots – The Saga of an American Family.* And later my love of storytelling was nourished by spending two days traveling with the renowned late actor Richard Harris, whose entertaining stories were nonstop — and many unrepeatable, at least in his original colorful language.

The ability to draw lessons from stories is a gift, as demonstrated in these pages. I particularly appreciated the author's willingness to be so remarkably candid in including stories that some might find a challenge to share. That, in itself, demonstrates that he possesses the "right foundation" to help us understand how leadership is not bestowed upon a person when they are placed in an important position, but rather that it is earned as a result of what they do to attract and deserve the respect of those they lead.

One of the aspects of Carson's book that I particularly appreciate is the way in which it reinforces how our personal and business lives are a compilation of stories. It is up to each of us how or whether we choose to apply the stories and lessons we have learned — from as far back as the 7th grade or as recently as our last work encounter. This book demonstrates how to use what happens in our lives, good or bad, as learning experiences and reminds us that this meaningful vantage point is especially applicable for those in positions where they desire to be both a boss and a leader.

The key step, in my experience, is to understand that every encounter you have in life (no matter how small or seemingly insignificant) helps form your unique story. And your story can create your destiny. So, pay attention to what is happening. Learn to listen and observe. Some of the best leaders I've known led by keeping their eyes and ears open to what was going on around them and what they could draw from it. And some of the worst leaders in my career were those who were oblivious to anything that might interfere with their own preconceived notions. They were right because they said so. They may have been the boss, but few of us considered them leaders.

Pay attention to what is happening. Learn to listen and observe. Some of the best leaders I've known led by keeping their eyes and ears open to what was going on around them and what they could draw from it.

A vital next step in improving your performance as a leader is to reflect on what you observe and hear in order to extract lessons that inform your leadership style and day-to-day decision-making. In this book, Carson wisely emphasizes the importance of cultivating a routine of reflection that serves two purposes: so the significance of an experience is not lost and so valuable lessons get absorbed and ultimately applied.

My hope is that you see yourself as you read this book, and that it helps you appreciate the stories all around you. And, I hope you are open to the lessons that you can apply to your life. The key is to be open — or as Alex Haley put it:

"When you clench your fist, no one can put anything in your hand ..."

———————————

Tim Doke is an accomplished strategic communications and marketing leader, and the founder and principal consultant at TJD Comm, LLC. He formerly served at the highest levels of marketing, communications and public affairs leadership at aviation, technology and healthcare organizations. He is perhaps best known for his role as the point person at American Airlines during 9/11 and other crashes, labor disruptions, and high-profile litigation.

INSPIRATION

Commit thy works unto the Lord, and thy thoughts shall be established.

– Proverbs 16:3

I have posted this Proverb on my computer monitor and in my prayers for years, and I'm continually amazed by the power the message enables. Times that surpass counting, I've had no solution or path forward then I've turned to these powerful words and gained clarity ... I've come to know the steps to take in my thoughts or through the people placed in my life's walk.

Surely, I am inspired by the words and promise of this Proverb. I am also inspired by the people to whom I am closest. I am inspired by my wife and life partner, Sandy, who supports and pushes me in her inherently genuine and thoughtful manner. Sandy continues to inspire me to be the person I was created to be and to stay true to the fulfillment of our shared goals. I am likewise inspired by my sons, Trey and Taylor, who have become wonderful friends to me as they have grown. They motivated me to write down the experiences and lessons I've learned (many of which I have passed onto them over the years), so that others could benefit through this book. I'm also blessed to have the support and love of my mom and dad, who gave me a wonderful start to life and provide continued support to this day. Lastly, I want to acknowledge the contemporaries of my family and former colleagues, who have validated the experiences and lessons I've shared with them as valuable.

DEDICATION

I humbly dedicate this book to all my family, colleagues, teammates, and friends along this career and life journey. I am so fortunate to have so many individuals who have created, challenged, and influenced me. I'm honored to have friends across the spectrum of demographics and geographies. I've learned and grown as a person through my relationships with people from the southern United States to New England, from Ireland to the Netherlands, from South Africa to Australia, and all points on the map in between!

This book has been written in my mind during the past 40+ years, and was finally brought forth into words and chapters during the quiet, lonely times I experienced while working away from home. In writing this book, I was warmed by the embrace of memories from everyone in my life, and the times we've shared. Together we experienced much — tackling difficult technical issues, addressing organizational issues, and, with the coaching of younger professionals in my life, working our way through a resume, interview preparation, or a challenge they faced for which I might offer a glimpse of clarity or support. All these moments are part of this book and my life!

And to all of you who are reading this book, who I have not yet met, I dedicate the stories, lessons, and foundational thoughts. This book was written for aspiring and developing leaders, and if you are touched positively, inspired, or provoked to reflect upon a course of action because of the investment in reading my book, I'll have been wonderfully successful in this endeavor! Thank you for reading.

INTRODUCTION

For me, a simple formula captures how life evolves:

Experiences We Live + Decisions We Make = Who We Are

First, thank you for investing your time by reading this book about the experiences and lessons I've accumulated over my life. It is my hope that you will find several stories, suggestions, and insights that will help you on your own path, saving you time or heartache (as you learn from my experiences and even my mistakes) or fast-tracking your career success (as you gain a sneak peek into leadership decisions and challenges that you might not face in the real world for many more months or years).

I've structured *Bosses Are Hired ... Leadership Is Earned* around a collection of stories because storytelling is a key tool in both leadership and personal development. As you jump from chapter to chapter, I hope you find these stories to be both entertaining and thought-provoking.

Each story in this book is titled based on foundational truths — the foundations I've developed for myself as a result of my experiences. In each story I share, I've focused on the key roles of a leader that I've observed, developed and employed in my career.

You'll hear a lot about me in the stories; however, I admit I'm still on my learning journey and it's important that you read these stories with the mindset that this book is about *you*. I believe I'll never stop learning, tweaking, and gaining from experiences in my life and work (both the good and bad). I hope you never stop learning either. For me, the continued learning is grounded by the foundation I established for myself. After 35 years of business leadership, it stands to reason that I have some lessons to share, so here we are. But I don't put myself forward as an expert. I'm just a person who has derived value from the experiences in my life, which I'm motivated now to share with others. I am honored to have earned the leadership of people, projects, and organizations across my career, and am thrilled to now be assisting developing and aspiring leaders on their paths.

Enjoy the stories, reflect upon the lessons, and shape your life and leadership journey so that you arrive precisely where you are destined to be — in leadership positions that are earned and not simply bestowed!

About the Title –
Bosses Are Hired ... Leadership Is Earned

Before it was my book title, it was a piece of wise guidance that I received early in my career, as the first story will illustrate. This statement, if you decide to own it, can define the level of humility required of yourself as you contemplate your future in any organization. And true belief that "bosses are hired ... leadership is earned" adds an important layer of context to the responsibility of a leader to make critical decisions and take appropriate actions that align both with the needs of the people in your organization and the goals of your business.

Many individuals perform and deliver on business expectations as a "boss" without the leadership endorsement from the team or organization they have been placed in charge of directing. Think about your own career. Have there been people with "boss" titles — like Manager, Director, Vice President, Supervisor — who were responsible for leading people, projects, and organizations, but about whom very few people would have said "Yes, he's a true leader" or "I am honored to be led by her?" If so, you'll appreciate the difference between being a "boss" and being a "leader."

One major differentiator between a boss and a leader is the sustainability of performance that a true leader can inspire. In the later phase of my career, I was interacting with an employee who was leaving for an opportunity that was a great career move for her. She made a statement that clarified for me the distinction between the "boss" and the "leader." She described my leadership style as different from what she previously had experienced. She said, "You've elevated the performance of our business and organization by lighting a fire *within* us, rather than lighting a fire *underneath* us." I was humbled by this description, and it gave me pause. When we light a fire within the people we lead, they are able to burn bright and perform at peak levels for a long time — even after we are no longer in charge. But leaders who light fires underneath their employees heat them up to perform once or for a short period of time, until that external fire or pressure burns out. True leaders inspire performance that can and will be sustained over time.

"You've elevated the performance of our business and organization by lighting a fire *within* us, rather than lighting a fire *underneath* us."

The delineation between a boss and a leader rarely can be defined by "the what" a person sets out to accomplish. Today, in any organization there are basic challenges: the delivery of continuous improvement, doing more with less, delighting customers, etc. There also will be "what have you done for me lately?" expectations from inside and outside, as well as up and down, an organization. The "what" we must deliver as an organization or business is defined and should be articulated clearly. And, any person in a responsible position who doesn't achieve the established targets could face a short tenure of time in their role. In today's environment, people are sophisticated in knowing their organization must achieve established goals.

The critical differentiator of "boss" versus "leader," in my experiences, is not "the what" but "the how." A leader not only invites people in the organization to contribute, but they will establish an environment where individuals are excited to be a part of the solutions and courses of actions established. Long ago, I heard a quote that has stayed with me, and I've seen it play out as true time and time again. "Tell me and I'll be informed; show me and I'll understand; involve me and I'll own the goal as my own!" While a boss (but not a true leader) is apt to respond to inquiries with silence or the much-despised "Because I told you so," this approach is unlikely to inspire success or earn a person's strong sense of ownership and commitment. It's hard to look up to or work hard for someone who hasn't earned your respect. On the other hand, a leader who asks you for your input and truly listens — or, better yet, acts upon your input — will solidify the value the leader holds for you and you for them.

Throughout this book, I'll share experiences and learnings from my past that illustrate the obligations of individuals who seek to be successful in positions of leadership. In reality, every person and organization is unique and requires an investment of time to gain valid insights on how best to lead. The ability to adapt successfully to the needs of an organization, matched with real clarity around the leader's foundational beliefs, will be key in driving an organization's performance.

The ability to adapt successfully to the needs of an organization, matched with real clarity around the leader's foundational beliefs, will be key in driving an organization's performance.

To complicate matters further, an organization is a living entity that is always evolving and changing. As a result, the tools available to the successful leader also must continually evolve and change. Early in my career, the sharing of a letter from a satisfied patient with my organization was highly effective. While sharing this format of feedback is still important, the introduction and presentation of actual patients to my organization elevated the insights and commitment of the people into the power of what we delivered. Tools such as "Net Promoter Score" elevated the precision of feedback, follow up, and client engagement to ensure we achieve the performance and delivery sought by them. On the other hand, while emails, texts, and instant messaging made communicating more accessible, the old school method of walking through the business, holding town hall meetings that include questions and answers, and even joining people for lunch still speak to the people in the organization the high value you place on them. Markedly, the experiences a leader absorbs, and the subsequent decisions made, will communicate strongly the character of the leader and ultimately the positive wake they can create.

The experiences I've had over decades — which form in large measure the story of a life — have helped me understand both the positive and negative contributions I have made to my family, my friends, my colleagues, my employees, my bosses, and, of course, my businesses. *Bosses Are Hired* is an effort to document some of my most impactful reflections and points of learning. Simplistically, I have learned that, at the source, the experiences we encounter and the decisions we make are fundamentally the building blocks of who we are as individuals.

Let's get into the experiences — the stories. These situations, and the decisions I've made as a result of them, continue to form the essence of my life as a husband, father, friend, leader, and person. The recognition of experiences I encountered and decisions I consciously made has influenced outcomes in every aspect of my life.

I'm hoping my stories connect with you in a manner to provoke your own self-reflection and ownership of who you are and how you can influence your walk of life, as well as others you encounter along your path. I've written this book over and over in my mind, throughout my life and career. My motivation to share simple areas of focus and foundations of leadership lifted from the decades of my career is borne by the prospect of helping you to reflect and develop your own (or adopt mine). The content captures the results of my self-reflections and assessments that I've routinely conducted on a nightly basis, since a pivotal night long ago when I was 12 years old (see Chapter 2).

Every workplace experience leaves lessons in its wake. As you read the pages that follow, ask yourself the following questions:

- What lessons might you have taken from these situations, had they happened to you?
- What can you learn from me and my colleagues?
- What would you have done differently or better?
- If you were to write a book about what you've learned in *your* career (or about the impact you hope to have in the coming years), what chapters would you include?

The opportunity to be labeled a leader, formally or informally, is truly a blessing in life, one to be cherished. The chance to positively

influence your organization and the people around you are irre-
spective of your role or title — remember, leadership is earned (not
bestowed with a fancy title or a corner office). Everyone can positively influence and lead, but like everything in life worth achieving,
hard work is required. Let's get to work ...

STORIES

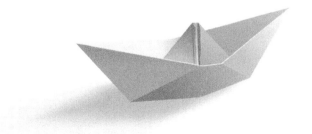

CHAPTER 1

Bosses Are Hired ... Leadership Is Earned

Early in my career, I was given a powerful truth: "Bosses are hired, leadership is earned."

I have used this introductory statement in every organization I've joined. People get it! Well, most do. (And if you're like me, you've got some painful stories about those who don't.)

Imagine a workplace in which those who invest time in understanding the concept of "earning" leadership outnumber those who don't — so one day "earned leadership" will tip the scales so that everyone in a position of influence grasps the difference between being hired into a position and actually leading in ways that positively impact their organizations. I'll confess up front, when a boss I've had didn't recognize the difference, I quickly realized that I would not be successful under such supervision. In these instances, I first prioritized my performance and the positive delivery of my organization. Honestly, individuals who don't recognize the difference are typically only interested in results. By delivering results, I earned the ability to provide feedback and coach upward. The absence of delivering results and providing feedback would place me in a position to be labeled as a complainer or not a team player.

In those unfortunate times where I failed at managing upward to affect a change, I initiated the process to find employment elsewhere (which happened a few times in my career).

Through experiences early in my life, I recognized disingenuous people, just as you probably have as well. To some degree, we all have an inherent ability to assess others as either genuine or phony. Think of this as a kind of BS radar that comes standard in today's business employee. In my first role out of school, the team I was designated to supervise brought their ability to the forefront.

After graduating from Wake Forest University in 1983 at age 22, I didn't immediately realize what was in store for me — or that another of the many lessons in leadership was headed my way! While working in a textile mill in the fall of 1983, I was put into a management trainee role that was designed to familiarize me with the processes and technology used to manufacture denim for companies like Levi Strauss and Wrangler. As it turned out, I was pulled from that program before it was complete and given a new assignment. I was to take on a recently vacated second-shift supervisor role in the department responsible for cotton opening and carding.

The processes performed in cotton opening and carding are the first manufacturing steps of making cotton yarn. In cotton opening, the process is exactly what it sounds like. Bales of raw cotton are arranged in a grid pattern based on the yarn's physical characteristics, fiber length, fiber strength and micronaire (air permeability when compressed). A robotic lift would select cotton from each bale and load it into hoppers to be conveyed to the card room, optimizing the strength of the cotton by blending the different bales together. In the card room, we didn't play cards! The name of the operation refers to the card machines that receive the raw cotton and begin the process of cleaning the cotton of twigs, bolls, etc., and initiating the alignment of the fibers. The additional processes in the card room continued to work with the cotton sliver (the precursor to yarn) to align the fibers and strengthen the cotton sliver through additional processes (drawing and roving) to deliver a strengthened and smaller diameter cotton sliver to be used in the next phase of manufacturing, spinning. Yep, this was as hardcore textile manufacturing as there was anywhere in the world, with a crew of 26 people ranging in age from 18 to 65.

My shift's start time was 4:00 p.m., six days a week, with one Saturday off each month. The 26 people who had just been assigned to be supervised by me included operators, cleaners and fixers. (Operators ran the equipment, such as a card operator was responsible for a set of eight carding machines. Cleaners continuously swept, dusted, and captured the loose fibers to ensure dust and debris in the work area was minimized. And the fixers kept the machinery running and in a good state of maintenance.) Outside of work, they were grandparents, parents, married and single people who were leaders in their churches, little league coaches, and volunteers in the community. In other words, the crew included people with significantly more work and life experience than me.

While this position was my first leadership role in my professional career, I quickly realized I was not the first supervisor who had been assigned to take care of their needs at work. I had shoes to fill, expectations to meet (or exceed or fail to live up to), and responsibilities to take on. After a first week in which I mostly focused on getting to know each member of the crew and learning what their duties consisted of, I recognized what the crew really wanted was to maximize output — while not pushing too much product into the spinning department (the next process of yarn production). One third of the crew was on an incentive-based compensation structure and the other two thirds wanted to ensure that those colleagues could maximize their earnings without alerting the industrial engineers. You see, the industrial engineers would raise the production requirements for incentivized employees who achieved output above the defined maximum, which I personally regard as a ridiculous approach to maximizing efficiency. There's nothing quite like punishing people for a job well done!

A Mentor from Among the Ranks

On a cool Thursday night, my head fixer Freddie came up to me and asked me to take a walk with him. Freddie was in his 50s and had worked in this cotton mill for more than 20 years, with a break in time to serve in the Army. Freddie knew the mill, the people, and how to run every job with ease. He'd achieved the top role in the company that he could reach without moving into supervision. He had chosen to remain as one of the "enlisted."

I walked with Freddie through the yarn staging area, down the three flights of stairs to the basement of the mill. He escorted me out the back of the mill, and he directed me to follow him out onto the old dam, which decades earlier had generated power to run the mill. As Freddie lit an unfiltered Camel, he asked me, "Do you want to be good at this?"

Admittedly, Freddie caught me off guard, as I'd assumed this walk was going to be another historical tour of the mill and the grounds to "show me the ropes." I responded to him with some uncertainty: "Depends on what you mean by *this*."

He patiently responded to my quip, "Leadership, not supervising, not being a boss. Do you want to be good at *leading* people?"

The genuine tone of his question clearly communicated his interest in having a serious discussion, versus some of the banter we previously had engaged in. Not knowing where this conversation was going, I told Freddie that I truly *did* want to be good, or even better than good! He smiled and nodded in a show of relief that I was interested in what he had to say.

As he lit another Camel with the one he'd just burned through, he looked me in the eyes and delivered the following advice:

> "Carson, you have a college degree, you've come to Western North Carolina to work, and you're now a member of management of this company. The crew and I have been watching you. We've seen your interest in the work we perform. You don't sit in the office. You're even attempting to learn how to do our jobs. We appreciate these actions, and we've all met and talked about helping you. The crew asked me to have this talk with you, and if I piss you off with what I'm going to tell you, it's on me and not the crew. Okay?
>
> I don't have a college degree, and I know being a lead fixer is as high up as I'm going to go. What I do have, however, is more than 20 years of watching and working for many supervisors and managers — the best and the worst of them. All of us on your crew can spot the bad ones and the good ones pretty quick. We want to share with you what we've seen, teach you how to help us be successful, because when we succeed, you will look good to the bosses! You may not realize it yet, but supervisors whose shifts deliver strong production numbers get promoted quicker."

I told him this all made sense to me, and I wanted to work with the team so we all could succeed. He replied,

> "Well, bossman [a mill term of endearment or sarcasm, depending on the tone], BOSSES ARE HIRED, LEADERSHIP IS EARNED."

He paused while I reflected on this simple but rich statement. And then he said:

"You and every boss I've worked for was hired into the job and took on responsibility for their crew. Whether or not you are honored by the crew to be called a leader is not up to you; it's up to us. We don't know what you want to do in your life, but we need you right now to help us to be successful. If you are open to the notion, we all want to help you to be the best bossman in the mill and to make our shift the best."

We shook hands, as we looked into each other's eyes, and sealed the deal for us to work together.

Over the course of the next two years, together with my crew, we exceeded in every key performance metric put in place by the business. One key measure was indicative of what we accomplished together as a team committed to everyone succeeding. Over the entirety of the two years, all 26 individuals never missed a day of work, setting a record of perfect attendance. I recognize that today, perfect attendance is not ideal, nor should it be a goal in itself. Back in the '80s, however, this achievement was recognized as special.

This single parameter is indicative of the commitment each person had for succeeding as a team, ensuring no individual went unsupported. If someone did need to miss work, their duties were shared amongst myself and the rest of the crew, which would have made for a difficult night at work and negatively impact incentivized individuals' income potential. From a business perspective, we worked out a solution to maximize output (number of hanks of roving produced, with a hank being approximately 850 yards of roving spooled on a bobbin), which increased the take-home pay for our team members on production incentives. As the team performed at their very best in terms of productivity and quality, we were able to maximize output, and we could begin the shutdowns earlier on Saturday nights to enable everyone to enjoy time with their families.

As a young person in my first career role, these two years were formative in how I would develop and who I would become as a leader.

 LESSONS LEARNED

The end of each story in this book will include a list of the key lessons I learned from these experiences. Be sure to take a moment to reflect upon how you can apply these lessons in your own career, how they might help fast-track you to improved relationships and new opportunities, and ask yourself, "What else, in addition to what Carson has outlined here, do I consider to be the 'morals of the story' I've just been told?

1. People understand the boss/subordinate relationship, but what they seek is a leader who understands three simple truths:
    - Everyone, regardless of their job title or duties, wants to be successful.
    - When subordinates are successful, the business is successful — and so is the leader.
    - BOSSES ARE HIRED ... LEADERSHIP IS EARNED!

2. Successful leaders provide specific and direct feedback in a respectful manner. They praise in public and critique in private. But just as importantly, leaders seek specific and direct feedback from their team.

3. If you are appointed or already hold a supervisory role, people listen to what you say. But more importantly, they watch what you do. A simple formula for success is:
    - My Decisions + My Actions = Trust

4. People want to hear the truth from their boss. Not all messages are what people want to hear, but they need to hear them all. Honesty is non-negotiable!

THE MIRROR TEST

Questions for Self-Reflection

1. Think back ... Have you ever worked for a boss who has no idea how to lead and manage people? What steps did you take to improve this situation and still be successful in doing your job?

2. Those with senior titles are not the sole proprietors of wisdom! Practice changing your filter as you interact with others by removing job titles and truly listening to the thoughts of everyone, no matter how much perceived power or influence they have. You will find rich and amazing thoughts.

3. Have you made an effort to practice giving feedback? Starting with positive and encouraging feedback is an easier initial path, and it will help you develop your skills in providing both positive *and* developmental feedback.

CHAPTER 2

It's What People Don't See

When I was 12 years old, I had a life experience that became
a formative lesson and an opportunity to make a decision regarding
what I expected of myself. Yeah, yeah, I know you might be thinking:
"Seriously? A profound life lesson from a pre-teen?"

Yep, the experiences that life provides can bring opportunities to
make our own decisions rather than allowing ourselves to feel victim-
ized or shortchanged. And, if you pay close attention, these learning
experiences are a constant in our lives. There's always another one
right around the corner.

In 1971, I moved with my family to North Carolina from Kwajalein
Island, which is located in the Marshall Atoll in the South Pacific.
This area of the world was a United States Trustee Territory that
housed military complexes and missile defense systems. As for
North Carolina, if you have any knowledge of this part of the world,
you'll know that, in North Carolina, the sport of basketball evokes
extraordinary levels of passion. I was introduced to the game when
I was in 5th grade, and I was fortunate to have decent height, agility,
and a love for competition. I fell in love with the sport and played
constantly with my friends in pick-up games and in church youth
leagues. I'd never considered the prospect of *not* progressing from
youth league to the school team.

In the 7th grade, we had tryouts for the junior high basketball team. Coming to the last cut of players down to the final roster, I already was looking forward to being a key contributor on the team. As Coach Clonz posted the final list of players who had made the team, we all gathered around the bulletin board. I was totally unprepared for what I was about to read ... or more specifically what I wouldn't read. I was not listed on the team's roster! I was crushed.

Whether you've been cut from a team, separated from a relationship, or let go from your job, over the course of life, you're bound to face an experience of feeling excluded or dumped. I can recall vividly the pain I felt in my gut, especially the embarrassment I felt at not being good enough to play formally among the friends who'd played together for the past two years. In my mind, I had placed a lot of who I was in being an athlete and now I faced the reality of this life-changing event. Not only did I have to face my friends and class-mates, but I would have to tell my parents that I wouldn't be a part of the school's team.

That night, I couldn't sleep and I didn't look forward to going back to the school and confronting the humiliation I felt. Sometime in the middle of that night, I caught a glimpse of myself in the mirror of the bathroom in the hall. I hesitated and stared into my own eyes as I asked myself a simple question, "Did you do everything you could have done to make the coach come to a different decision?" What I recognized was that I couldn't lie to the eyes that were reflecting back at me in the mirror. I honestly answered the question. "No."

I'd gone through life to this point with success coming naturally, just because. I recognized that my life had suddenly shifted to a new realization that I was not physically or mentally able to be successful without additional investment and commitment. I made a promise to myself in front of that mirror to be able to reply in the future to the eyes looking back that I had done *everything* I could to achieve the goals I've set for myself. I was learning the value of discipline and hard work, though I don't know that I was mature enough to call it that.

I made an appointment the next day with Coach Clonz to get his advice on steps I could take to make the team in the future. We had a tough conversation, but one that has marked me throughout life. He told me that he had put a lot of thought into whether or not to keep me on the team. He said his final decision rested on whether I had the potential to contribute positively to the team. He had based his decision on the actions he had observed throughout the tryouts and in school.

He told me that I had a great opportunity to be successful (or not) in life based on how much or how little I invested to succeed. I told him I wasn't clear on what he was saying, and he gave a specific insight. He said he sought players who not only can shoot, rebound, and handle the ball, but he looked also for those he could count on when the team faced adversity. He asked me to recall my performance at the end of each practice, as we ran suicide sprints after we were already worn out from two hours of drills. He said he had observed me "dogging it" during these sprints, which told him I hadn't put in the time outside of tryouts to be the best I could be for the team.

The last thing he said to me that day has stuck with me throughout life:

> "Carson, you will be judged by your performance when the lights are on and there's a crowd in the stands, but what will make you successful in sports or life is what you do when no one else is watching."

You will be judged by your performance when the lights are on and there's a crowd in the stands, but what will make you successful in sports or life is what you do when no one else is watching.

This experience and the decisions I made following this one disappointment enabled me to achieve success both in academics and sports — and ultimately in business. Being human, I've continued to experience times in my life when I jeopardized my goals by not investing myself fully when the "lights weren't on." However, I've always pushed myself and taken great care to consider the effort and energy I invest in the goals I want to achieve.

In life, we all experience disappointment, but if we self-evaluate and reflect honestly, the decisions we make following those disappointments will define who we are in life more fully than the experience itself.

 LESSONS LEARNED

1. We always have a choice to blame someone else for unfair circumstances. But in doing so, we relinquish our lives to the control of others.

2. The one person you cannot lie to is looking back at you in the mirror.

3. Listening to feedback from others is a gift to cherish and use. What you do with the feedback is a choice you own.

4. Hard work and personal investment can overcome the limitations of your talent, enabling you to be the all-star of your life!

THE MIRROR TEST

Questions for Self-Reflection

1. Take a look at yourself in a mirror ... Can you honestly say you are striving to be the best person you can be, and striving to make those around you be successful as well?

2. In the face of disappointment, have you reflected upon your own actions and what you might have done differently to change the outcome?

3. We all face rejection from others in our lives. Take the opportunity to learn about the basis of the rejection from others to gain insights into how others see you. Doing so will enable you to define who you are, while not accepting a view from another as the only view.

CHAPTER 3

Good Bosses, Great Leaders

During my career, I've had the great fortune of working directly for several very good bosses, who I also considered to be great leaders. I've learned a great deal through my experiences with them and through a lot of good, old-fashioned observation. In many ways, they were so sharp and so agile at what they do that those of us watching them and benefiting from their mentorship could mistakenly think that leading an organization and a business is an easy thing to do. (You've all heard it said, "They make it look so easy!")

Watching and emulating, however, don't always go hand in hand. Observing the leaders I have worked with is analogous to watching a professional athlete perform their craft. Sure, I watch Professional Golf Association (PGA) tournaments, and the swings appear so easy and smooth. But watching is a far cry from doing. PGA professionals are able to generate imperceptible power, which only can be appreciated — and envied — by amateurs like me.

Watching is a far cry from doing.

So now that I've shared a couple of stories (and related lessons) with you, let's take a step back for a moment to take a close look at what good leaders look like — how they behave, how they communicate, and how they lead ... in good times and bad. Perhaps you're reading this book after only having had the benefit of one or two bosses in your career. Maybe no one who you've reported to at work rises to the level of someone you'd deem a true "leader" — someone who has earned your respect and loyalty. So you might be wondering, "How can I become an outstanding leader if I've never even met one?"

It's a fair question, and the world of work is unfair in expecting aspiring and developing leaders to know how to excel without great role models. For that reason, I'm going to do my best in this chapter to share a series of experiences I've had with leaders I admire. The leaders I highlight in the next several pages weren't chosen because they were "successful" (even though they were). Remember that a lot of mediocre bosses, too, ultimately achieve success in their career. What I want to share are my reflections as to why these particular individuals in *my* career demonstrated the "IT" factor — that something special that makes me want to thank them and applaud them, all these years later.

A cautionary note: The great leaders I've had in my career are those with whom I had balanced and respectful relationships that were developed and valued by both of us as workplace partners. The partnerships formed were, at least in my eyes, the key to our individual, mutual, and organizational successes. Like a lot of people, I don't enjoy being "told" what to do, which evokes an immediate reaction. Good leaders, however, are able to define and shape job requirements as opportunities! To accomplish this, the boss and subordinate have to put away their respective self-interests and accentuate humility to ensure the partnerships are good for each other and for the organization.

Jim

My first boss, after achieving my first "adult" job following grad-uation, was a good boss and is still a good friend. While Jim and I haven't worked together for decades, we did work together at two different companies early in my career. The magic sauce that Jim brought to the partnership included the following traits:

- Jim had the ability to articulate clear objectives to illustrate what success looks like for the business and for my performance.

- Within the boundaries of safety, quality, and any legal implica-tions, Jim supported different approaches and creative solutions, not just to achieve our objectives but to surpass them. And, there was no micro-managing!

- Jim engaged me in idea generation and provided growth options beyond the scope of my role. His ongoing tendency to involve me in opportunities outside of my shift benefited him and his short-term decision making. And for me it was an unexpected chance to gain valuable knowledge and experience.

- Jim allowed me to make mistakes, but he never let me fail. This one trait impacted me as much as any, and I carry with me today Jim's example as I work with individuals, partners, teammates, and colleagues. In contrast, I've worked with others in leadership roles who seem to delight in the failures of others with various and questionable motivations. Interestingly, I've never seen a single one of that type of leader deliver a successful outcome for the organization.

- Lastly, Jim was always able to provide me with critical feedback that kept me from making significant mistakes, with the under-standing that the failure to course-correct would be on me and I would own the consequences.

What a great start to a career! Throughout our time working together in the cotton and hosiery mills, Jim and I enjoyed wonderful success. Beyond the lessons I learned in my everyday conversations with Jim about work and the organization, Jim taught me the value of continuous improvement. When I would come into work ahead of my second shift crew, Jim occasionally would have an idea he wanted to run by me. Often his ideas, and his experimentation with different approaches to the manufacturing of cotton roving — the process step just ahead of spinning cotton into yarn — was scoffed at by the long-time lint-heads as ridiculous!

Jim's quest to look for new approaches — without the fear of them not working out — excited me. What a way to approach the job ... bringing your team together to challenge the status quo, to design experiments, to learn from ideas that didn't work, and then to keep at it!

Jim also was career oriented, and he bestowed his own desire to develop, learn, and progress in his career upon me as well. His interest in his career included interest in developing me and others in his organization. Jim recognized the power of succession planning for both his direct reports and himself. I learned from him, both at this first company and when we worked together at the next organization, that you have to own your career development. You simply can't afford to sit back and wait for someone higher up to pluck you out of a sea of employees and place you on a promotion track. You have to own and earn that yourself!

You simply can't afford to sit back and wait for someone higher up to pluck you out of a sea of employees and place you on a promotion track. You have to own and earn that yourself!

Walt

Walt came into my life after a shift in my career, and just when I needed another mentor to lead me. After eight years working in the textile industry, with six years of that time spent leading the human resources function for different manufacturing sites, I needed to change industries. The textile industry's footprint in the United States was diminishing as manufacturing was being off-shored. Jim, that first good leader I just profiled, had been key in pulling me from front-line supervision in the cotton mill into a personnel role, which was a grind, but a terrific opportunity. While learning the human resources profession, I was also charged with staffing the 1,200-employee hosiery business, which (based on many factors) was experiencing an annualized 80% turnover rate. The experience and resume I had built from working six years in human resources provided a career bridge into another industry.

Back in the 1980s and early 1990s, the route to find different opportunities was to scour the Sunday newspaper to look for job opportunities in your field. My wife Sandy and I would buy Sunday papers for towns and cities around the Southeast to look for opportunities to submit my resume, in hopes of getting a call.

The job search process has evolved dramatically over the years, but certain elements remain the same. Specifically, very little has changed about the roller-coaster ride of receiving a call and an onsite interview, only later to receive a rejection letter and maybe some well wishes. One Sunday, Sandy came across a small two-inch ad in the paper for a Director of Human Resources. The advertisement didn't identify the company, so I wasn't immediately comfortable with submitting a resume. Sandy convinced me to do so anyway, which was just one of many times Sandy has had a profound and positive influence on my career.

Lo and behold, I received a call from the recruiting firm that placed the ad.

Now this is the point in time when Walt came into my career and life! Walt was instrumental in my successful transition from textiles to pharmaceuticals as his new HR director.

Today, as I write this profile about Walt and remember our time working together, I'm smiling as I think about him! Walt is one of the most brilliant people I've ever known. He is a mathematical genius, but most importantly, he demonstrated the value of knowing what his strengths were and what strengths he needed on his team to cover areas where he could leverage fresh talent. Walt brought the following traits to his leadership:

- He had confidence in his knowledge, experience, and abilities — yet was humble regarding areas where he wasn't as strong.

- Walt invested time not only in learning from his subordinates, but in developing any of their areas of weakness. We spent many hours in the operation, where Walt taught me the business from every vantage point — the science, the technology, the financials — helping me understand what drove pharmaceutical manufacturing.

- Walt was focused on the team and invested time in forming the team. Each person had a role; however, together we were expected to be one unit as a leadership team. Walt saw the value not only in working together, but also in investing time away from work to form relationships based on shared off-work experiences.

- Walt would invite others to earn the chance to perform in the spotlight. This meant leading from the front when needed, but also being comfortable with letting your team members shine on their own.

- Walt appropriately showed his emotions, from a fiery temper to genuine and heartfelt care for the people and the business.

- Walt placed a high value on intelligence, which he believed comes in all shapes and sizes.

- When a conflict arose in the team, Walt consistently would side on the best path forward for the team and the organization.

Walt would invite others to earn the chance to perform in the spotlight.

Walt's hiring me, in conjunction with the North American Director of Human Resources (who would be my functional boss), opened up a whole new world for me and my career. Having previously worked only in the textile industry, I found it eye-opening to see the pharmaceutical world's investments in tools, training, and interaction with the local and broader team.

While hard to believe today, I was amazed by everyone being outfitted with their own desktop computer, having multiple printers in the facility, and even multiple fax machines! At my previous employer, we had owned just one desktop computer for a site of 1,200 people! Walt took time to ensure I understood the organization, his network, who he relied upon, who he listened to with guarded filters, and who he simply would ignore. He also provided valuable insight about his relationship with his boss, who Walt admired and held in high regard. Walt reported to a man named Bobby — and the opportunity to observe how he and Bobby worked in a boss/subordinate relationship, but also as peers, was a great development opportunity for me.

Over time, Walt ensured I had opportunities to interact with individuals from across the business, and he secured for me a spot in the first leadership conference for our business. These were exciting times in a business that had completed one of the era's most successful mergers between two major companies (not just in the pharmaceutical industry).

The merger of SmithKline and Beecham was later chronicled by the *Harvard Business Review* as a blueprint for managing the combination of two equally strong companies. I was fortunate to have Walt place me in a position to be an eyewitness and participant in the integration of the activities of these two businesses.

I'll always cherish a conversation I had with Walt regarding the development of the organization and ideas I had presented to him regarding a change in the structure. Walt had led the manufacturing site in Aiken, South Carolina, for 15 years, and he was comfortable with the structure in place. I presented him with the concept of reorganizing the site into focused factories, versus the current structure that was organized functionally around groups like a manufacturing department, two packaging departments, quality control, engineering, and maintenance.

Looking back, I perhaps was naïve and a bit bold to come to Walt's office and propose that we totally restructure the site. To Walt's credit, he challenged me with the simple question, "Why change?" Fortunately, I'd experienced some rejections in the past (both for well-thought-out proposals and others not so grounded in true potential). As I presented my structure proposal for Walt, I explained the possible positive impact on turn-around time, total quality, and financials, with the caveat being establishing end-to-end ownership of full product lines by the teams.

Walt could have dismissed my proposal, as a plant manager had done years before in my career (see Chapter 5). But, because of his experience and knowledge, Walt did not. He coached me through a series of questions regarding impact, implementation, disruption to the business, and, most importantly, selling the idea to my teammates on the site leadership team.

During eight years of working together as boss and subordinate — and later as colleagues on the global leadership team for our sector of the business — Walt supported my development and growth, and also admitted he had learned and developed from me. We held countless town hall meetings, faced immeasurable challenges, even respectfully removed some fellow team members when the business had outgrown their roles and ability to contribute.

By 1999, when Walt made the decision to retire, he had played a pivotal role in supporting my promotion to lead the site. While it was unheard of for someone from HR to take over a Site Director role in the pharmaceutical industry, Walt's development of me and his accepting me as a partner in leading the business paved the way for me to take on this role. As testimony to Walt's leadership, I recall the first town hall meeting that was held to introduce my promotion to the Site Director role from which Walt was retiring.

Lena, who worked in our packaging department, made this statement during the Q & A portion of the meeting, "Carson, you are no Walt!" I'd known Lena for years and held her in high regard. While the statement was made with humor and brought a point of levity in the meeting, it gave me an opportunity to acknowledge the truth of her statement and to commit to welcoming feedback from everyone in the site! And importantly, I was able to acknowledge I was, indeed, no Walt, but I believed we could all be successful by working together.

Over the subsequent years, I can't remember how many times leaders in the pharmaceutical industry asked me to explain how someone from HR could take on the leadership of a manufacturing site, especially without a technical or scientific degree. While

I typically responded by explaining the experiences I had invested in to develop and learn, I know in my heart it was because of Walt!

Rob

A number of changes took place in the organizational structure of SmithKline Beecham in the mid-1990s. A handful of years before Walt would retire, Bobby, Walt's direct supervisor, retired. My functional supervisor in Human Resources was promoted into a different area of the business. The closeness of Walt and Bobby could have set up a difficult transition for Walt, me, and the overall site Walt led in South Carolina.

Before I move on with my reflections regarding Rob, I need to provide a couple of points of clarification because I acknowledge how confusing it can be to hear a story about three guys named Rob, Bobby, and Bob! Walt was my site director and direct boss, and he reported to Bobby, who was the vice president of manufacturing. I reported to Bob with a dotted line, and he was my functional boss for HR. Rob, who is the subject of this section of the book, replaced Bobby when he retired.

Rob was appointed to lead the Consumer Healthcare manufacturing organization in the U.S. and Europe, where Bobby had previously been responsible for the U.S. sites only. Rob's approach to introducing himself to Walt and the organization established a smooth transition from the first day. Rob appreciated how well Walt ran the South Carolina site, and had done his homework regarding Walt's capabilities and accomplishments as a leader.

He acknowledged these traits in Walt right from the beginning, and he shared his appreciation for knowing Walt's leadership of the South Carolina site would allow him to focus more attention on the larger network of more than 10 sites located in the U.S. and the E.U. Rob was also experienced in leading pharmaceutical sites, having led the company's site in Cape Town, South Africa, in his past.

Following a period of orientation, Rob quickly engaged with all the sites. However, he spent quite a bit of time understanding the consolidation work underway at the South Carolina site and a site in the UK, which were designated for expansion. During his visits to our facility, I was able to interact a lot with Rob and ultimately Rob promoted me to replace Bob, after he had been promoted. Bob was also instrumental in my being appointed to help Rob lead the HR function for the U.S. sites, and I will always be grateful to Bob for his support of me.

In time, Walt also retired, and my work with Rob and Walt resulted in Rob's appointing me to the site director role of the South Carolina site. As I've stated previously, the career progression from Human Resources to the Site Director role over a pharmaceutical manu-facturing plant was atypical. Rob recognized my experience, capa-bilities, and connection with both the South Carolina site and the corporate organization as a natural career path for the leader of one of his largest sites in the network.

Rob's leadership style was unique and I learned a great deal from him. I consider him a great boss and leader for many reasons, including those below:

- Rob evaluated individuals at face value, not based on the roles they held. If he saw potential, he found opportunities to develop the talent in those areas.

- Rob was hands off, but always supportive and open to listening to the needs of his team. He would expend political capital to help his people gain access to resources necessary to operate the sites within his network.

- Rob invested a lot of time in developing the individuals who reported to him into a team. He made sure the geographic separation of his team was not a barrier to forming the relationships necessary to support and challenge one another.

- Rob rarely led from the front, preferring to place his team members in positions to showcase their skills and talents, while he coached in the background.

Rob rarely led from the front, preferring to place his team members in positions to showcase their skills and talents, while he coached in the background.

Anton

Anton and I worked together as boss and subordinate after I had been the Site Director of the Aiken, South Carolina, pharmaceutical manufacturing site for almost three years. He was one of two fine gentlemen from South Africa who I've been honored to work directly for in my career. Rob ultimately made the decision to promote me to lead the manufacturing site, following my supporting him as head of HR. And when Rob retired, his colleague Anton took over the leadership of Rob's sites in the U.S. and the E.U., along with retaining leadership of all sites located elsewhere in the world. Anton had a huge organization of more than 20 sites that manufactured and distributed medicine to our commercial segment of the corporation.

I'll always remember the news of Rob's departure with sadness. When changes in leadership take place, the loss of someone such as Rob has the potential to derail the direction of the business. Anton's appointment to replace Rob, as it turned out, was a blessing. Fortunately, I'd gotten to know Anton over the past few years, and he was clearly the best selection to lead this significant part of the corporation's business. Upon hearing the news, I reached out to Anton directly. I welcomed him, told him I looked forward to working for him, and said I anticipated the opportunity to share with him the progress we were making in my business in South Carolina.

His response, gracious and polished in line with Anton's character, expressed his enthusiasm for his new responsibilities and the formation of his leadership team. There was a specific comment he made to me that remains in my memory still: "Dear Carson, I too look forward to working with you and our getting to know each other further. And, I expect us to work *together* rather than you just working for me."

How powerful it was for Anton to acknowledge that he is my superior on the organizational chart, but that his focus would be on working collaboratively. During the ensuing years in which we worked together, I never lost my respect for his superior position, and I was driven by a desire to deliver success for him and for the people who worked in my organization.

As I learned early on in my career, *Anton was appointed my boss, but he earned the right to lead me.* I fully invested my experiences, capabilities, and intelligence to ensure he was successful. You often hear how true leaders inspire their organizations to achieve success. Well, that is Anton!

Anton's leadership captured those traits I'd seen before in Jim, Walt, and Rob. Beyond those wonderful traits, Anton shared with me his learnings from experiences in working in an international corporation.

- I'll always be grateful for Anton's investment in me to elevate the level of gravitas and situational awareness in my thinking. Anton's meteoric rise within the company had exposed him to the nuances of the political maneuvering within the corporation and he openly used his experiences to develop me.

- He was masterful in his encounters with adversaries whose objectives often were not aligned with what Anton considered the best course for the business, our employees, or ultimately the patients to whom we provided medicine.

- Anton drove me and my colleagues to elevate the performance of our sites, even sponsoring healthy competition between us for growth opportunities and capital investments. He had the fine sense to use the competitiveness among his teams while leading us toward being unified around the goals that we commonly held and were committed to.

- He used everyone on the team to progress the business, with equality among us and showing no favoritism. Even though our individual organizations were located across the globe, Anton brought us together as one team that not only achieved outstanding results, but also developed close personal relationships.

Laura

I met Laura for the first time on my 50th birthday. Laura served on the interview panel that evaluated my candidacy for the leadership and turnaround of a large pharmaceutical contract manufacturing organization in Eastern North Carolina. I had previously interacted with the CEO of the pharmaceutical division of that corporation during several interviews for the prospective role. I had already developed an admiration for the CEO, so I was looking forward to meeting the team in Eastern North Carolina and seeing the business.

The primary goal of the role was to lead the business in North Carolina through a transformation and elevation of its performance to enable the parent corporation to sell the pharmaceutical business. Laura was the leader of the commercial organization, which included sales, marketing, project management, and all points of interface between the manufacturing organization and the business's clients. The clients included many large and well-known pharmaceutical and biotech companies around the world.

I recognized during the interview with Laura that I would enjoy working with her as a colleague on the leadership team. Fortunately, I was hired to lead the operations and manufacturing part of the business and to work in partnership with Laura and her commercial team. Our partnership began immediately, and Laura was a key resource for my gaining insights and understanding of both the relationships with our clients and nuances of the organization in general.

We aligned on the need for change, and we recognized the changes would be bolstered by our partnership. In the early days of our working together, I shared with Laura that she was a large contributor to my excitement in joining the team and the business. Further, Laura played a pivotal role in my learning and development regarding the intricacies of contract manufacturing and working in a business-to-business (B2B) focused entity.

Laura and I both reported to the president of the pharmaceutical business. He was a brilliant individual in the areas of science and technology surrounding the manufacturing of finished products for biologic and pharmaceutical formats. With respect to organizational leadership, however, he experienced difficulty engaging with the organization. Not long after I joined the leadership team, he left the company, and Laura was promoted to president and elevated on the organizational chart to being my boss instead of being a colleague.

The dynamic of changing positions from colleagues to boss and subordinate can be difficult. In this situation, the relationship Laura and I had developed in the months leading up to her promotion provided a healthy foundation for the change. Beyond that foundation, Laura's experience, capabilities, and style enabled her to transition into the lead role seamlessly. As we met following the announcement, Laura was very straightforward in recognizing the change in roles and responsibilities, while sharing her desire and need for us to continue to work in partnership as we had during the preceding months.

Laura and I didn't have the opportunity to work together for an extended period of time. Our corporation was successful in selling our business. Laura moved into another executive position with the new owners and I ultimately left the business after leading the site in North Carolina through the transition to the new company. However, her leadership was a positive influence on the business and organization. Namely (and consistent with other great leaders) Laura's approach as a partner in her leadership style allowed for both of us (and our organizations) to be successful.

As mentioned earlier, Laura's experience in negotiations and interactions with clients were highly valuable in developing my knowledge and understanding of the nuances of the B2B world. Specifically, our relationship with the clients was always a balance of give and take, ensuring the clients were kept informed of any issues in supplying their products from the operations I led. The products we supplied included the most expensive drug product in the world (which was a biologic drug) and we became the entire manufacturing arm of another large and successful pharmaceutical company that had strategically outsourced all its manufacturing to us.

While there were many successes, Laura and I faced a particularly contentious situation with a client — a situation that had resulted from the poor quality performance and supply of a key product for the client's portfolio. As Laura laid out the strategy for a meeting designated by the client to communicate their plan to exit our business, she provided me with great feedback on positioning the plans I'd put in place to improve the performance of the business. The specifics of informing the client about how the plans would be executed involved a commitment on our part to provide specific updates and metrics on progress. The improvements in our organization's performance, and the consistent reporting of key metrics (and sometimes issues encountered and steps taken to resolve them) improved the relationship with the client. Within less than two years, the client actually recognized our business with their top supplier award and the most improved supplier award.

I will always be grateful for lessons I learned from my time working for Laura, both professional and personal.

- I had never worked in a business-to-business (B2B) situation, and Laura shared with me her experiences and knowledge of working directly with clients. Specifically, she modeled how to spend appropriate time to truly understand the key expectations of the clients.

- Laura fully supported me and the other members of our team. I watched as Laura used her influence to ensure talent in the business was recognized, even if they had been disregarded by other senior-level employees.

- Laura introduced to me the importance of the Net Promoter Score tool, and most importantly, openly following up with clients who provided feedback through personal follow up.

- On a personal perspective, I saw how Laura handled her personal life and work life balance. It is tough to work during the week (and some weekends) away from your family, but Laura provided a positive example of how to make this situation work.

 LESSONS LEARNED

1. Great bosses give you the freedom to make mistakes, but they will not allow you to fail.

2. You have to own your own career and development. Passively waiting for something to happen or for a "big break" to fall in your lap will stagnate you.

3. Know your strengths but be humble enough to admit your weaknesses. Use this knowledge to build a team that covers all the bases. Develop your weak spots, while building on your strengths.

4. To build a team, you have to invest in being a team. Yes, you need common objectives and goals, but you also need experiences shared together that are outside the confines of the work environment. In short, you need to focus on building relationships.

5. Leaders who focus on the development and growth of their subordinates also grow and develop from their team. Good leaders are constantly developing and growing their organization's succession plan.

6. Leaders can create an environment of healthy competition within the team, while maintaining solidarity toward the goals of the entire team and the business.

7. Leaders can coach and develop you by how they conduct their lives, both in the workplace and personally.

THE MIRROR TEST

Questions for Self-Reflection

1. Have you ever had a boss or leader who made it all look so easy? Have you learned more from their leadership style, or from someone who has to really work hard at becoming a successful leader? What are the greatest lessons learned from each style?

2. Consider ... Who in your life do you consider to be a great leader? With them in your thoughts, write down why you believe they are a great leader, and consider what traits they demonstrate that you can adopt as your own.

3. Have you experienced the joy of being part of a great team? What steps were taken to make the team great? How can you use these steps to build *your* team to be a great one?

CHAPTER 4

Leadership Can Be Lonely

On January 11, 2008, I was awakened by my phone ringing at 5:24 a.m. The voice on the phone simply said, "Carson, get to the plant, now!"

Half asleep and hearing these words, I attempted to get more information from the caller, but they had already hung up. I quickly dressed and headed to the plant site in the dark of the early morning, not knowing what I would face when I arrived. I had worked at the site for almost 17 years, and I was the site director for almost nine years at this time. The people and the business were dear to me, so the uncertainty of what I was going to face was powerful.

The psychological impact of the unknown manifested itself physically throughout my body. I could feel electricity running through me and I had a physical feeling of dread within my core. As I came around the bend in the road before getting to the business property, I saw the eerie glow of red and blue flashing lights reflecting from the road and the trees. As I approached closer, the lights also reflected across a white lump lying on the ground at the edge of the site property. *"Oh, God ... please tell me that's not a body,"* I thought. I parked my truck, closed my eyes, and prayed for strength and wisdom to be the leader my people needed.

Fran, our head of security, rushed to me to say that two individuals had been struck by lightning during a cigarette break at our designated smoking area. One person was injured and the other was killed by the strike.

How in the world does a leader react to this news? I caught my reflection in the side mirror of my truck, and I felt a separation of my heart and mind unlike I'd ever experienced before. As my brain took over, I assessed the situation and quickly formed coherent thoughts about the actions that needed to be taken. It was nearing 6:00 a.m., and the first shift of 250 people would be showing up for work within the next 30 minutes. I asked Fran to have her security team find all members of the leadership team who were on site and have them join me in the engineering area. Now.

I scribbled some notes about the message I would deliver to this team, and how to ensure we were able to separate our own emotions and thoughts from the challenge we were facing. As the local leadership team gathered, the anguish and stress were so strong you could actually see and feel it in the room. I told the team, "We will have time eventually to grieve and to explore our emotions, but right now our employees need us to show them compassionate and decisive leadership." Heads nodded. I told the team that we were shutting down the operation, and we needed to speak personally with each person arriving for work and also with those who were already on site and would be leaving from the night shift in a matter of minutes.

I positioned each member of the leadership team in pairs at the three different entrances to the site and assigned two to communicate to the third-shift crews. I gave them three specific messages to deliver to each person, because we needed to be direct and ensure we could control the situation as much as possible.

- We are shutting down operations today.

- We have experienced a tragedy on our site.

- We will be providing updates on the company hotline and through supervisors regarding what the future operations schedule would be.

The team took the direction and went out to manage the immediate need to evacuate the workers on site and keep the oncoming crew away from the plant. Standing out in the dark on a rainy January morning, it was important for the leadership team to have clear and concise direction on the actions to take and words to use, which gave them a valuable source of focus. As each worker was met at his or her car, the team did a great job in turning people around. By 7:15 a.m., the only people left on the property were security, leadership, and emergency response personnel from the city and county. The injured individual was transported to the hospital, and another ambulance removed the deceased.

During the next hour, it was critical for the employees of the site to be updated, and to take actions to help manage this tragedy for our people. The leaders of the plant and other personnel who were required to be on site to manage the shutdown also needed direction. I asked everyone on site to meet in the cafeteria at 8:00 a.m. As the meeting began, I requested we observe a minute of silence. I consciously allowed the full minute to pass, which felt like an eternity, but the emphasis of this time was what we all needed to allow our emotions to play out. After this pause, with tears streaking down all of our faces, I delivered the following message:

> "Thank you to each of you for managing the safe evacuation and shutdown of our site over the past two hours, despite the sadness and questions we all are experiencing. I have no script or specific training for what to do in such a situation, what not to do, or what our next steps should be from this point forward. But I have

confidence in our collective ability to define the steps we need to take in leading our people through this tragedy."

We then brought out a flip chart and began brainstorming all the actions we needed to take, the communications we needed to manage (internal and external), the resources we needed to employ for our team, and the timing and schedule of how and when we would resume the operation. We talked about our need to be at the hospital with the family of the injured person, and the need to visit the family of the deceased. We agreed on the message to cascade to our people regarding what had taken place at our site. While we were all in shock and managing our own emotions, together, we mapped out a plan to lead our organization through this tragedy.

While we were all in shock and managing our own emotions, together, we mapped out a plan to lead our organization through this tragedy.

The rest of that day was a blur of activity, speaking with our corporate leadership, the local press, our Employee Assistance Plan resources, OSHA, and our employees. It was a Friday, and we decided to call every employee back on site the following Monday at 9:00 a.m. Bringing all shifts together and allowing us all to meet and share in our grief and shock was important; we needed to let the healing process begin.

Come Monday, we had a team of grief counselors on site and available 24/7 for people to talk with as needed. We allowed this day to be about us as humans, before we restarted the business on Tuesday. Over the coming weeks and months, some employees sought counseling, but mostly we relied upon each other. The injured employee's condition improved, but an event such as this one always remains. We ensured the required and needed services were provided to her, as she healed physically. Members of my leadership team and I attended the funeral of the employee who passed away, and we ensured we covered all expenses associated with the funeral and more.

One of my lead team members, Joe, also did a lot of volunteer work at our local university. He was the announcer for multiple sporting teams. He came to me with the idea to use the same lightning warning system the school used to ensure no one was outside when storms came. He researched the tool used and wrote a policy for us to adopt it at our site. Going forward, we ensured no one would be exposed to the potential of a lightning strike again. As a matter of fact, I made it a practice of implementing the same technology and policy in every business I led after this incident!

 LESSONS LEARNED

1. Organizations respond to the leader. If a leader panics, the organization panics. If a leader is calm, the organization is calm. As a leader, you sometimes have to be able to separate yourself from your feelings.

2. When facing extreme adversity, simple instructions allow people to focus and contribute.

3. Any organization is a sum of individuals who become connected as a single being that will pull together or apart on the basis of how they are led.

4. The resilience of a team will be tested and these times of testing will form the character of the organization and its leaders. This character ultimately is reflected in the performance of the business.

THE MIRROR TEST

Questions for Self-Reflection

1. Have you ever worked for an organization that has experienced
    a workplace tragedy? Were you counseled and spoken to honestly
    about the tragedy? What would you do differently as a leader, or
    a future leader, if you were responsible for responding to a crisis?

2. Emotions are part of the human experience, but how we let
    situations or other people influence our emotions is up to us.
    Consider times when your emotions were evoked to a level that
    bursts from you. What thoughts or mechanisms could you use to
    share positive and inspiring emotions, while suppressing nega-
    tive ones when the time is appropriate?

3. Tragic events are an inevitable part of life and work. How you
    react to these events will impact others around you. While
    it's admittedly tough to do, what steps or actions can you take to
    develop a sense of calm and support to help others?

4. Consider the fact that when you're in a leadership role, behind
    every pair of eyes that's watching you directly are even more
    eyes watching and depending on the people on your team. What
    steps can you take to consciously stay aware of the impact of your
    actions that reach beyond your team?

CHAPTER 5

Organizations Deserve the Truth

I went to work with a hosiery company in 1985, after working as a front-line supervisor in a cotton mill on the night shifts. I was hired to be the second most senior personnel leader at a large hosiery site in Eastern North Carolina (before the Personnel Department was called Human Resources). In 1986, I was promoted to lead the personnel function at a smaller hosiery mill outside of Greensboro, North Carolina. In November 1987, I was promoted to Head of Personnel for a large textile manufacturing site in Tennessee. The facility was a dominant feature in the downtown of this eastern Tennessee community. It was also the largest plant in the corporation, and leading their personnel function was an opportunity that my wife and I agreed was a good career step for me. The site produced high-end fashion hosiery for women, and it had been in operation for nearly a century.

It wasn't just the site that had been around for a long time — many of the employees had held roles for literally decades. The plant manager was in his late 60s and had been the head of the site for nearly 25 years. In the beginning of my tenure at the site, I spent a lot of hours out in the factory, getting to know the people and learning the business. On my own, I would study the financials of the plant's business performance. Well over 1,000 people were employed there, and I had my work cut out for me to meet them all and to learn the layout and operation.

During my first few months in the role, I repeatedly ran into aspects of the business that didn't line up with information I had been given from the plant manager. In our discussions, he consistently shared the plant's virtues of success and delivery. He shared with me how well he was connected with the organization, and the fact that he had a strong insight into the organization and the people.

In contrast, I saw the operations producing a significant amount of stock that was going through re-inspection or being discarded as waste. I observed people not working consistently in an efficient manner. I was too young in my career to diagnose specifically the disconnects I was observing versus what I was hearing from the plant manager. But I knew there were issues that weren't being addressed.

I was fortunate to find a group of individuals within the company who, like me, were early in their careers. We connected with one another in the early days at the site and would periodically meet for lunch or coffee to talk about life and work. We shared our observations and our concerns regarding the viability of the plant. Some of us were well attuned to the challenges the textile industry was facing. Many firms in the U.S. were shifting manufacturing away to countries with lower wage and benefit costs.

After several discussions, we decided to spend some intensive time together to work through the opportunities the organization had to improve performance. This was a time in the U.S. when Lean, Six Sigma, and other quality management tools either were not known or discussed. What we did have available were some individuals trained as industrial engineers who were at the forefront of the early stages of Lean thinking.

Together, we came up with a plan for engaging the workforce and improving quality, eliminating waste, and measuring our performance so the entire staff would have visibility into how well (or not so well) the business was doing. We also began investing time with different groups of employees to discuss what tools they needed, and what ideas they had for working smarter instead of harder. As a group, we were excited about the prospect of taking on this challenge. We knew we had many hurdles to cross, but we were committed to go for it.

The biggest hurdle, unfortunately, was the plant manager, who would have to buy in to some or all of our plans. If we embarked upon implementing our plan without his knowledge and endorsement, he would stop us in our tracks. Because I was positioned in the most senior role of the group, I accepted the challenge of selling our plan to the plant manager.

My Best, Futile Effort to Effect Change

From my short experience and interaction with him, I knew the best time to approach the plant manager and request a meeting was during his morning ritual of sitting in the cafeteria while he was drinking coffee and smoking a cigarette. He had told me previously that he knew everything going on in the factory by being available every morning in the cafeteria. He said he had many contacts in the factory, and they came to him during this morning time to share their thoughts and ideas. In reality, he was merely holding court with people who told him what he wanted to hear (and not necessarily the truth) to ingratiate themselves in his eyes.

To make my request for a meeting look right, I started my own routine of going to the cafeteria at 6:00 a.m. for several weeks, and I made sure he saw me there. As he became accustomed to my presence, and because he apparently liked the fact that I was in early, I approached him to request a meeting, which he accepted for a few days later.

In advance of our meeting, I studied, memorized the numbers, and I itemized the opportunities that my small group and I had identi-fied to improve the performance of the site. As I entered the plant manager's smoke-filled office, I was confident that he would receive our plan well and, ultimately, would appreciate our initiative to improve the site's performance. I started by explaining that I had been studying and learning our business, and that I had connected with a number of managers on site to explore different opportunities to improve performance.

WOW! I barely finished my opening statement when the plant manager slammed his hand on top of his desk and yelled, "What in the hell do you know about this business? I've worked here 40 years and I know everything that goes on here! I know our performance, and I don't need some young up-start [my words, not his ... which were more colorful] coming into my office and telling me how to run this plant. Get the hell out of my office and stick to your job, and you had better tell your college-educated buddies that you're not going to tell me how to do *my* job!"

I took a deep breath and walked out. I admit I was young, and the old man was a master of intimidation, but I also was confident. After taking some time to re-group with my colleagues to come up with a different approach, we agreed we would implement a small part of our plan with one department in the plant to collect actual results from our plan. As we met with the members of that department and asked for their ideas, a true excitement started building about what we could accomplish together. After the initial improvement ideas were identified, implemented and delivering benefits, I was charged with taking the evidence back to the plant manager to seek his endorsement and support. *Here we go again.*

As his secretary ushered me into his office, I recognized from his facial expression and body language that this conversation, like our last, might not go well. I started by telling him about the steps we had taken with one department. I started to share with him the statistics of performance we were tracking.

Not long into my explanation, his face turned bright red and he exploded, "Get the hell out of my office! You may have a college degree, but you just proved how stupid you are! I told you NO, and you went behind my back anyway. Now leave, and don't come into my office again, unless it's an emergency!"

I was angry, frustrated, and the only response I could come up with was, "This *is* an emergency; you just can't see it!" I walked out the door, knowing I had to leave this plant location as quickly as I could to keep my career on track and to support my family. I felt power-less to effect the change the organization needed and deserved. On a personal front, my wife and I were expecting our first child, and we had made the decision to be a one-income family. The prospect of losing a job because of this dinosaur hit me hard. From a professional perspective, this position was my biggest role in my short career. The prospect of failing would potentially derail my career before it really got going!

I decided that I needed to reach out to senior managers in the company who had already promoted me twice. Fortunately, I received a warm reception from the VP of Personnel, who said he had predicted I would end up in conflict with the plant manager. He and the VP of manufacturing had moved me to Tennessee in an attempt to gain insights into what was truly happening at the mill. Well, they got their intel from me. Fortunately, I was able to transfer back to another site for the same company in North Carolina. Unfortunately, the site in Tennessee continued to perform poorly, and within six months of my departure, the plant closure was announced. I volunteered as part of the team to meet with the employees who worked there to share with them their outsourcing benefits. To say it was a difficult week would be an understatement.

Sadly, the loss of the major employer in this small town rippled well beyond the employees and their families. As I met with employees who were losing their jobs, I couldn't help but be both saddened and angry. I still felt quite sure that this failure didn't have to happen, or surely not as quickly as it came about. One stubborn man had hurt a thousand and beyond. It didn't seem fair because it wasn't.

 # LESSONS LEARNED

1. People in an organization need to be informed about how the business is performing. In the case of this particular manufacturing plant, providing truthful, tough messages could have allowed the people who relied on this plant for their livelihoods to have made the necessary changes. While it only might have delayed the final outcome, at least they would have had a fighting chance.

2. Never underestimate the impact of ego, or the fear of change in some individuals. The plant manager, who had been very successful for decades, took the proposal for change as a personal affront, ignoring what the business needed. In difficult situations, sometimes good people with decision-making authority just make bad decisions.

3. Recognize what you can change or influence, and focus your attention on those areas. For aspects of work or life that you can't change, simply accept them and become effective in how you deal with them.

4. In every life or career, there will come a time when you have to make personal decisions for your own welfare and that of your family. In this instance, I saw the disaster that was coming, and I reached out to the broader organization for opportunities in other parts of the business. One of the saddest duties that I had was volunteering to return to this site to perform exit interviews with as many of the employees as possible following the corporation's decision to shut down this old factory. It felt like an "I'm sorry" along with a "goodbye."

Never underestimate the impact of ego, or the fear of change in some individuals. In difficult situations, sometimes good people with decision-making authority just make bad decisions.

THE MIRROR TEST

Questions for Self-Reflection

1. Have you ever worked for a boss who led using fear tactics? How did you react, and was this person a successful leader? Were people loyal to this boss? If so, why?

2. What steps have you taken to learn different aspects of your business, or even just what other departments or teams are working

on? How can you make sure you don't get "siloed" in your organization?

3. Facing rejection is tough, but you can learn from those tough experiences. How do you prepare yourself for the potential of your ideas, opinions, or proposals being rejected?

CHAPTER 6

Leaders Have Issues Too

Over time, I learned that a career in leadership inevitably meant there would periodically be situations or events that leave you at a loss for what to do — situations with no precedent and no way to anticipate anything quite like it. Alas, another one of those "Now what?" catastrophes took place, forcing me to think on my feet and act with confidence and speed.

At the time of this newest catastrophe, I was leading a large biologics manufacturing facility that I had agreed to lead for a period of two years. I committed to leading the organization through a transformation that would result in enhanced performance across a range of critical key performance indicators. As the business was experiencing growth, it also was facing future challenges from a competitor that was investing heavily to introduce themselves to the market.

Our site was hiring people in all areas, and we were implementing a re-organization of one of our major divisions. After just under a year of leading the business, I could see that the metrics weren't where they ultimately would rise to, but the trends were going in the right direction. Importantly, our people were energized and engaged in the journey we had embarked upon.

Around that time, one of our newly hired senior leaders came to visit my site as part of his orientation to the company. We held very engaging meetings, and I admit I was excited about the vision he shared with me and the positive impact he could make on my site and organization. I thought, *"This guy is a good guy and a bright guy. Things are looking up."*

Because my role was intended as just a two-year assignment, I was commuting back and forth to this facility from South Carolina every other weekend, while renting an apartment in the downtown area just minutes from work. The commute was tough, as the site was located in another region of the US, and I had to connect flights in either New York City or Washington, DC, to get home and then return on the following Monday. I left work one evening to go back to my apartment, feeling good about the trajectory of the business and the new senior leader I would be partnering with on our journey of continuous improvement, which by now was in full swing.

Another Unexpected Phone Call

I had gone to bed and was sound asleep when the phone rang.

When you lead a large manufacturing organization and the phone rings in the middle of the night, it's never good. The call was from my director of operations. She hesitated and fumbled around with her words, as I was attempting to focus my mind out of the fog of sleep. I finally asked her simply to tell me what happened.

She bluntly responded, "The police have called and they have the new senior leader in jail!" I asked for her to repeat what she just said. I heard her clearly enough but I needed to buy some time to think. After she repeated what she told me, I asked her specifically who was called and who knew that this individual was in the local jail. She told me security was called, and they reached out to the night manager.

The night manager was out in the plant, so it took a while to find him. (I remember nodding and smiling just momentarily, glad to hear he was out on the floor with the people, rather than hiding out in his office. That would be my only smile of the night.)

Once reached and informed, the night manager called the operations director and asked her what we needed to do. What she decided to do was to call me. She proceeded to tell me that the local police would allow us to come and pick up the new leader from jail, and she wondered what we needed to do at this point. I asked her to call back the night manager and the security officer on duty and instruct them not to disclose any information about this incident to anyone else on site. I asked her to make sure that the incident report was put into an envelope and handed to me when I got to work the next day.

I assured her that I would take care of picking up our new colleague from the jail. I sounded more confident than I was. I was new to the town, and I had no idea where the jail was even located! I knew where City Hall was, so I got dressed and walked the three blocks to the building. No jail!

So, by this time, it was after midnight, and I did what anyone else would have done first (before going for a walk!). I Googled the location of the jail and discovered it was nearby but further than I cared to walk. So, I got in my Jeep and drove to the jail. I found legal parking around back, walked into the building, gave them my business card, and explained I was responding to a call that my business had received from the police. In other words, I was there for the drunk guy (as I would soon learn).

The receptionist went to get the officer, who invited me into a private office to talk. He told me that they were holding our new senior leader, and that he was significantly intoxicated. He said my colleague had caused such a scene at a local bar (after the bartender refused to continue serving him) that the police had been called.

The officer went on to explain that my new co-worker — the guy I had just recently been so impressed by — was so drunk and belligerent that they had to handcuff him and bring him to jail. He said the guy repeatedly told them who he was, who he worked for, and what role he had for the company. He was proudly bragging about how important he was. Apparently, he was also so threatening and abusive that it required multiple police officers to handle him.

And here *I* was, wondering how I'd handle him. In the end, the police officer with whom I was speaking said that he and his department had great respect for our company and appreciated all that we did in the community, and he said we could handle this incident "off the books" as a courtesy — as long as we made sure our new "leader" never caused another scene in this town. I assured the officer that I would address the situation, and I would make sure the man was delivered to his hotel to sleep it off. As he brought Mr. Drunk and Disorderly to me from the holding cell, it was immediately apparent that he couldn't walk straight. I watched him struggle to put on his socks and shoes, but didn't offer to help. I did, however, help support his efforts to walk to the Jeep.

When I got into the Jeep, I quickly rolled down the windows to evacuate the stench of him. Fortunately, the ride to the hotel was a silent one. I couldn't think of a single thing to say. And he was apparently smart enough to know there was nothing he could say to make this better. Upon reaching his hotel, I asked him if he needed help getting to his room, and he mumbled that he was fine. As he exited the Jeep, he asked me where his briefcase was. I told him there was no briefcase, and he needed to get to his room and sleep it off. I told him we would discuss this in the morning. (I never did find out what became of his missing briefcase.)

The next day, I ensured that anyone with knowledge would hold
this event in confidence and I personally sat down with the head of
security and told him that I didn't want the incident report to be filed,
given that the incident didn't happen at work and because filing an
official report would make this after-hours dirty laundry available for
others to view. We agreed and, ready to put this all behind us soon,
I waited for our new senior leader (hopefully sobered up by now) to
come to work and for us to have a talk.

Surprising to me, but evidently not to those who worked for him
and were waiting on his arrival, he showed up a little after 9:00
a.m. despite the fact that we were an early-morning kind of crew.
I approached him and told him that we needed to talk. He told me he
would come see me in a little bit, which didn't set well with me. After
an hour, we went into my office. I started the conversation by telling
him that sometimes everyone has a moment, and that I've taken
steps to manage the situation confidentially at the site.

To my surprise, instead of expressing remorse or embarrassment for
his behavior, or gratitude for my professionalism, he immediately
went after me! He asked me, "Why did you pick me up from jail?" He
raged for several minutes about how much I didn't know him, how
his personal life was none of my business, and that he was being
targeted with an arrest and a "conspiracy" because of his "beliefs"
and his "personal life." I had no earthly clue what he was talking
about, or why his anger and paranoia were aimed at me.

WOW! Just 24 hours ago, I had thought this guy would be great for
the business and to work with. But clearly, he had serious issues.
I looked him straight in the eye and told him, "I know what drunk
looks like, smells like, and sounds like, and you were drunk! What
you do with your own time is your business. Unfortunately, when you
decided to drag our company's name into your personal business,
you made it my business. This town is a small one. Our company is

a significant employer in the community. You came to my facility, and you brought this behavior to the community where we work! I have to consider whether or not I need to provide a head's up to my boss to ensure he is apprised of the situation. Whether he decides to share the incident with your boss is his business. I have an obligation to ensure my boss is not blindsided by an event that I didn't share with him."

He responded, "You don't have to worry about communicating to anyone. I'll tell people who need to know what happened!"

The story continues, of course, because all train wrecks are long and twisted, but let me jump to the conclusion. As a result of the kind of corporate politics I'll never appreciate, this person was able to spin the situation with key executives in the company. He came out smelling like roses instead of bourbon. And those who were in the know about that fateful night were inevitably mistreated and even suspiciously exited from the business. I was astonished.

For the balance of my two-year tenure with the company, there were ongoing situations influenced by this guy that, had I not intervened, could have impacted my site, our organization's financial delivery, and our relationships with clients. I was required to attend multiple meetings in which my part of the business was challenged with inaccuracies by the most senior levels of our company, and I believe I knew the source of the misinformation. As I knew my business in detail, I would push back with facts and data to counter this misinformation. While these types of interactions were not atypical, a specific conversation tied it all together for me. As I sat with my boss (who was a peer to the subject of this story) during a performance review, my boss told me, "Carson, the work you have done in this site is great and you are exceeding our expectations. We are pleased to see that the results of the transformation are ahead of the timeline we discussed in your interview. I do need to tell you that, as good as you are leading your site and organization, you have to improve how you manage upward in the organization. You can't challenge the most senior leaders in our company in meetings! Carson, you are not helping your career with us by challenging the senior leaders."

I was pleased that my boss recognized the good improvements the people in my organization were making, but the last bit of feedback came out of nowhere (or did it?). I had respect for my boss, and he was as good of an operational manager as I had encountered in my career. I also knew that he was a good soldier who would follow the instructions he was given, even if the instructions were misguided. I responded to him with a question, "Do you realize next week will be the 18-month mark of my two-year commitment?" He paused and responded, "Carson, has it already been 18 months?" I told him that next week would be 18 months, and the people in this site had already exceeded the improvements targets we talked about during the interview process. Further, I explained that if I don't challenge inaccuracies and plainly false statements made by the most senior officials, my silence would be an acceptance of what they are saying. I cannot and will not accept falsehoods. I reminded him I had been up front with him since we first met — that I wasn't interested in a career with this company, but that I did care deeply about the site, the people there, and our clients.

I remember saying to him, "I do respect you, and I know you will need to report our conversation back to your boss. If you guys decide my tenure in leading the site is over, I'll accept that decision. Further, know that I'm exploring my next opportunities but that I remain committed to the two years we agreed to when I was hired."

Ultimately, I fulfilled my two years with the company. We had a wonderful transition to the new site leader, and I appreciated the opportunity to say goodbye to the people at the site over the final weeks of my tenure.

LESSONS LEARNED

1. Some individuals can achieve significant positions of influence despite integrity flaws.

2. Assessment of leaders and talent is an inexact science, and character flaws can manifest themselves at unexpected times. How you react as a leader or a person when these character flaws surface is all you can control, so worrying about the actions of others who you don't influence is a drain of energy and simply unhealthy.

3. Unfortunately, politics is played at every level in every organization. Your radar has to be tuned to the nuances of words and actions, while not allowing yourself to read a conspiracy into every situation, but remaining conscious of the multiple layers of maneuvering that can take place. It's a balance that requires experience as well as the recognition that your view of a workplace situation is likely to sometimes be inaccurate. Regardless of how awkward the situation, you have to verify or challenge your thinking. It is better to address than to assume — at least some of the time!

 THE MIRROR TEST

Questions for Self-Reflection

1. Have you ever worked with or for someone who had an obvious character flaw? It can make for a miserable work environment.

What are some actions you can take to minimize the impact this may have on you personally or on your career?

2. How would you prepare yourself to properly respond to a colleague, friend, or even a superior who behaves inappropriately?

3. What tools do you have available to determine if the behavior of another will negatively impact your team, organization, or business?

4. Politics within an organization are a fact of life. Likely you will one day be the target of a politically motivated attack (though hopefully you won't). What steps will you take ahead of time to prepare yourself to fend off the attack or to bounce back from it quickly?

CHAPTER 7

Believe in What You Do

No matter where you work — large corporation or small business, nonprofit, government, or in your own venture — believing in the organization and what it delivers is vital to creating an atmosphere for success. Your belief has to be genuine, which you may have already learned from reading other stories in this book. Faking such belief and trying to lead are doomed to failure; the people you work with will tune into their BS radars to see your convictions as valid or not.

No matter where you work — large corporation or small business, nonprofit, government, or in your own venture — believing in the organization and what it delivers is vital to creating an atmosphere for success.

Believing in your organization includes believing in the products and services you sell. At one point in my career, I made it my mission to help others in my charge truly care about and believe in the products we manufactured. Our company made a number of over-the-counter medicines, vitamins, and a range of consumer products, all of them beneficial to millions of people in myriad ways. But being in the supplement business, we didn't make any specific product that was necessary for life. Or, that's what we thought!

Shortly after taking over the lead role for the organization, I received a handwritten note on beautiful stationary from a customer who used one of our products. The product, Beano, is an anti-flatulent that contains an enzyme to break down the proteins in beans and green vegetables, which can create gas in the digestive system.

> *Here I need to veer off the subject to express my appreciation to our marketing colleagues who devised an internal campaign for Beano, just for fun. They distributed a limited number of t-shirts that had the Beano logo on the front, but on the back there was a picture of a dog with the caption, "Stop blaming the dog!"*

Back to the experience. The letter was sent by a woman who was in her 70s and lived in a retirement community in Arizona. She wanted to express her appreciation to the makers of Beano for giving her life back to her. She shared that she had become a recluse over the years and had stopped participating in any social activities or gatherings held in her community for fear of the embarrassment of experiencing a fragrant or auditory gastronomical event in public.

Fortunately, her daughter shared with her the benefits of Beano, and she trusted her daughter's recommendation enough to try the product. Beano worked wonderfully for her, re-opening her life to interact and socialize with her friends and the community. For some, our products really *were* "necessary for life!"

Of course, sharing of this letter with the organization was an opportunity I could not resist. I read the letter in the Town Hall we regularly held to keep everyone informed of the business's performance. In our city, we weren't the only big manufacturing business that employed huge teams of employees. Those other businesses — both of them larger than us — produced passenger vehicle tires and toilet tissue. So there was a bit of a "team" rivalry in town, regarding which manufacturer you worked for. As such, I introduced the letter during my Town Hall remarks by admitting that tires and toilet tissue are certainly important products, but our ability to positively impact people (such as our retired letter-writer in Arizona) is life changing.

I couldn't help but think that our capacity to make such a collective positive impact on individuals in our society gave us the opportunity to see our work as something beyond a job or a career; helping others was a calling. As simple as this story was to share, it was important to take a moment to acknowledge that what we contributed with our everyday work truly had an impact on other people's lives. And, thanks to this customer letter, it had been elevated in our conscious-ness and positively influenced our motivation to achieve higher and higher levels of performance.

I couldn't help but think that our capacity to make such a collective positive impact on individuals in our society gave us the opportunity to see our work as something beyond a job or a career.

Investing Fully, Achieving Collectively

Years later, I was once again — and far more personally — affected when I learned that the contributions of yet another of my employers had a profound impact on the world. At that point in my career, I was working for a company that produced what are known as biologic drug substances (i.e., the active ingredients for biologic drugs intro-duced by pharmaceutical innovators). A dear friend of mine was fighting cancer. Richard and I were especially close, and had taken vacations together with our families, camped and fished together with our sons, golfed, enjoyed holidays, and even co-chaired the fundraising effort to build an activities center for our church.

At this time in my life, I was commuting back and forth to another region of the United States. I was committed to leading a transformation of the site that manufactured biologic drug substances, and my wife was supportive of this less-than-ideal arrangement. (On a positive note, we enjoyed the opportunity to explore another part of the U.S. that we had never experienced when she would fly to see me, versus me flying home for a weekend.) I had flown home for the Thanksgiving holiday in 2015 and was quickly reviewing my email between family festivities. I saw an announcement that mattered to me in profound ways. There was news that one of the biologic drug substances we manufactured at my site had just been approved for advanced renal cell carcinoma, which was the cancer my friend was battling. I immediately forwarded the announcement to Richard, letting him know about the newly designated indication for this drug, Opdivo. Within two weeks, he had an appointment with his oncologist to discuss the drug and, within four weeks, he was outfitted with a port and began his treatment.

A few months later, I was participating in a business dinner in Switzerland when my phone rang. It was Richard calling, so I stepped out of the restaurant to take the call, not sure what news I was about to hear. What I heard was an exuberant friend, who told me that he had not felt so good in years. He said he just called to say *thank you*, and to ensure I shared his gratitude with the organization that made his improved condition possible. I was excited for my friend, and I couldn't wait to share this positive experience with my organization. To deliver the positive news of my friend's wonderful reaction to the drug we manufactured, I shared a video Richard's wife Kathy had shared with me of him leaving the hospital to go home! The video was not great quality, but the message of the importance of our work hit home with everyone!

During my career, I've worked for many companies, and I've invested myself fully in the mission of every single organization because I believed in what we accomplished collectively. *"OK,"* you might be thinking, *"What if I'm one of the employees who worked at the tissue plant, or the tire plant you referred to earlier in this story? How do I connect my beliefs to the mission of my company or organization?"* While I am very blessed to have worked with companies that make life-enhancing and life-saving medicines, I was also proud of (and believed in) the work we did to manufacture hosiery. As a matter of fact, I still prioritize Burlington Socks as my "go to" brand because I know the quality and care the employees put into every pair manufactured!

Whether your organization produces a product or delivers a service, the ultimate value of the combined effort of each worker is immeasurable. Conversely, if you struggle — after contemplating your work — to see its value and to align yourself with the greater purpose of the organization, you should consider other options. But before taking this alternative course, consider how positively you can impact both external recipients of your company's products or services as well as your fellow colleagues. Think about the end-user of your organization's output (the customer, client, the patient, the student, the stakeholder). Think about the benefits that you or your colleagues can derive from being a positive member of the team. And consider the impact you may be having on the lives of others — strangers and loved ones alike.

Whether your organization produces a product or delivers a service, the ultimate value of the combined effort of each worker is immeasurable.

Courage Under Fire

Belief in the work you do isn't just a "nice to have" for workplace morale and for when times are good. One of the most consistently difficult tests of your beliefs occurs when an organization is faced with a plant closure or a reduction in force . Your personal beliefs are critical to helping elevate performance in the face of challenge, rallying everyone around a common purpose to show the worth of the organization and potentially reverse the decision made to negatively impact a site or an organization of people.

I recall in the early '90s being taken aback by a newscast that included footage being broadcast live from two auto manufacturing plants, one of which would find out by the end of the day whether it would be closed. As I reflected upon this situation, I deeply felt the predicament of the people who relied upon their jobs to support themselves and their families. I understood the pain of uncertainty.

I wondered whether this same scene would be playing out had the leadership of the organization presented the potential of this decision a year, two years, or even five years earlier. If employees at every level had been given a chance to collectively improve organizational performance, would the closure be necessary at all? I went so far as to share my thoughts about this situation in a Town Hall meeting, where I was addressing my own employees. I did so not to scare them or to intimidate them, but to highlight that we each have today to make a difference in our tomorrow! There are no guarantees anymore, but everyone can have a positive influence on the future of their organization by the commitment and investment they make every day.

There are no guarantees anymore, but everyone can have a positive influence on the future of their organization by the commitment and investment they make every day.

LESSONS LEARNED

1. To be a leader, you have to be able to inspire. To be genuinely inspirational, you have to believe in your business, organization, or team. In short, if you're not inspired by what you do, you won't be able to inspire and lead others.

2. It is vital to connect individuals to the whole (the whole team, the whole organization, the whole industry ecosystem, the whole mission). One attribute of a successful organization or team is the ability to see how the collective results of everyone's efforts deliver what could never be delivered by one individual, or even a machine. As we are facing the growth of artificial intelligence in our world, the differentiation of the combined focus and investment of people working toward a commonly held belief will become more and more important.

3. Leaders must create an experience that people buy into and believe. How do you want your colleagues or team members to describe what they and their organization do when they are having dinner with family or friends? A leader has to provide information and experiences for individuals to grab onto and own. Everyone seeks a sense of purpose. The opportunity to contribute to a mission that is genuine and believable is a critical step to achieving the goals of any organization.

4. The "what have you done for me lately?" attitude in business has always been in place, but the timeline to answer this question continues to compress. Every day (realistically every hour) can make a difference, so leaders must inspire their organizations to act daily in accordance with this reality!

THE MIRROR TEST

Questions for Self-Reflection

1. Are you working in a job that inspires you? Do you feel like what you do impacts people's lives in some way? Most all jobs make a difference in someone's life. You have to be observant enough to see it and take pride in it. Take time to be proud of what you do!

2. When you join an organization, you're excited about the new opportunity, learning new things, meeting new people, and contributing to the mission. How can you keep that excitement about your organization, the mission, and the team going? How can you mentally capture the exciting image of walking through the door for the first time available to replay it over and over in your mind?

3. Think about and prepare yourself to describe what positive contributions your organization makes at a dinner table with family or friends. How would you describe how your organization's products, services, or mission impacts your approach to your work and contributions?

CHAPTER 8

A Culture Exists: Is It the Right One?

After having read some of the stories in this book and taking a moment to consider the lessons learned, you may easily recognize a simple truth: **Very rarely are people the problem.** The corollary to this statement: Success is developed through people, not in spite of people.

Throughout my career, I have endeavored to act based on what I call my "leadership foundations" and have done my best not to arrogantly assume I'm always measuring up to my own standards. I have eagerly solicited and received feedback about whether I'm standing firmly on those foundations.

As a reader of this book, you too are welcomed to assess how I've done when it comes to the leadership principles I hold dear. In the "Leadership Foundations" chapter in the second section of this book, I'll take you deep into a conversation about those foundations and what they could mean for you as well. For now, know that my five leadership foundations are the following:

1. Actions + Decision = Words *(The trust equation)*

2. Honesty is Non-Negotiable

3. Feedback is *the* Essential Tool *(To receive, give)*

4. Every Individual Wants to Be Successful

5. The Ideas Are Here

Being a strong leader in the eyes of those I have led means so very much to me. So when a departing employee of mine, headed to a new opportunity and a good career move, shared the following unsolicited feedback, it was quite special. Her name was Tara and she said: "Carson, you've led our organization by igniting a fire within our hearts versus lighting a fire underneath us to get us to move." This feedback, like all feedback received, was a gift. In reflecting upon Tara's observation and compliment, which I rated as genuine from a departing person who had nothing to gain by inflating the ego of the boss, I was driven to consider what it really means.

1. What does igniting a fire inside of someone's heart look like?

2. How does one person influence another to stretch themselves beyond their comfort level?

3. How does a leader gain ownership for the success factors of a business from the people in the organization?

4. How does a leader unlock the ideas and creativity held in the minds and experiences of the people in the organization?

The answers to the questions above are obviously varied and unlimited; however, there are some simple points that are critical in shaping an organization's culture into a catalyst for business success. Fundamentally, everyone wants to do well and be recognized for their contributions. Individuals also want to be listened to, not just heard. These two success factors require a leader to be genuine and for him or her to dedicate significant time and energy in the organization. In my experience, the existing culture in the business is in place for valid reasons (whether the former or current managers see it or not). The reality about culture is that there is one, for better or for worse. The question, then, is whether the culture is the one you want and that the business needs to be successful. There will not be a successful future without a thoughtful analysis of the present. To understand the current culture, and to subsequently formulate a strategy and plan to adapt, change, or build upon what is in place, leaders must first diagnose and understand why the current culture is in place.

Fundamentally, everyone wants to do well and be recognized for their contributions.

I have previously shared that I was fortunate to take over the leadership of a large biotech business. The first series of Town Hall meetings I held there gave me a clear picture of the steep proverbial hill I would need to climb to gain inroads into the stoic regional culture I had been warned about. I had several barriers to overcome. Namely, I was an outsider from the South, and I didn't have direct experience in the Biologics Drug Substance manufacturing sector. I had been hired to lead a transformation of the business across all levels of performance: financial, quality, and safety. The opportunities for this business were tremendous; however, the people who worked in the business were not fully connected between departments and teams to work interdependently. The silos of the organization were an issue. Sure, the people were very competent and experienced, but each group's performance impacted other groups' work. The sense of transition of output from one area to the next was not always clear, which hampered the entire organization from operating in the rhythmic manner necessary for large manufacturing sites. The lack of alignment of the organization had evolved over the years as the organization grew rapidly, and a lot of the historical intimacy of the organization was lost because it was not focused upon in a tangible manner by management. In my estimation, the organization had lost its soul and sense of purpose; and in a bit of a draconian way, observing the inner workings of the organization felt like watching people just go through the motions of finishing another day.

Following my initial Town Hall — where I introduced myself as the new boss, shared some details about who I am as a person, and provided insights into what I expect of the organization and what the organization should expect of me — I invested significant time in the organization. I met individuals in the cafeteria, at their workstations, and most importantly in the operations and the utility/maintenance centers. I spent time in the operations on the night shifts and on weekends. I was seeking to find two key ingredients to the culture that was in place:

1. **Who are the organizational leaders who are not evident from studying the organizational charts?** Every organization has leaders who are unidentified as influencers to the culture of the business. Unfortunately, these individuals are often listed as "disruptors" or pains in the butt by management. In truth, these unidentified influencers are the keystones to gaining the forward momentum of change and transformation.

2. **What "organizational relics" are evident that point to initiatives that were not followed up on by the organization?** In every business I've led through a transformation, the influence of past investments in third-party consultants can be found (like graphs on the walls that are out-of-date). Management (corporately or locally) has nearly always invested — at some point in time — in some fad or initiative of the day, elevated a level of excitement in some of the people, but lacked follow-through or ongoing commitment to the initiative. In each case I've uncovered (and true in this business too), relics of past initiatives can

be found. In short, I've found it better to never have initiated a change than to initiate and let it fade into the "dark hole" of corporate initiatives. Fundamentally, there are some individuals who buy into the initiative and/or change as champions, while there are always others who are the detractors who say, "Here we go again!" The unfortunate outcome of not following through on initiatives or being consistent to a new approach provides fuel for the detractors to prove their, "I told you so!" predictions.

Unidentified influencers are the keystones to gaining the forward momentum of change and transformation.

From Observation to Action

After those initial Town Hall meetings, I felt ready to create a plan for action, instituting several key actions that I believed could engage and re-engage the organization. Those actions addressed areas of focus that were both tangible and emotional.

Tangible	Emotional
Translate **financial performance**, so the organization could not only see, but understand opportunities that were being missed every day. Ensure everyone knows the impact they have on positively contributing or detracting from the financial performance.	Without making excuses, openly discuss the financial performance of the business and the positive or negative impact financial delivery can and will have on the security of everyone's job.

Tangible	**Emotional**
Assess and identify **quality issues**, then connect the dots for the organization between these points of failure and the impact upon sustaining clients and gaining new clients. Additionally, connect quality performance to patients (beyond the clients) to solidify the personal impact of the work.	Bring patient stories to life in collaboration with clients, and seek personal stories from within the organization where family members were positively impacted by the quality of our work.
Fully invest in **safety performance**, specifically, ensuring everyone has ownership of their personal safety and the safety of their colleagues.	Engage employees in the safety journey, so they are active participants in watching out for each other, empowering everyone to pause before acting, and proactively engaging in identification and elimination of unsafe conditions, practices, or behaviors.
Activate **continuous improvement**, not just inviting participation, but motivating people to take risks in bringing forward ideas.	Publicly and privately address failed or lapsed continuous improvement efforts with the organization and the leadership team.

Tangible	Emotional
Define and map out the schedules and structure of interactions with clients, and identify designated points of contact for each client and their capabilities.	Identify strained or troubled **relationships** with the business and clients, and determine the root cause and what gaps existed between our client's expectations and reality.
Assess and understand the **investments being made in the business**; capital, development, and culture.	Determine and align strategies and procedures to fully leverage investments for optimum return, and identify quick wins to demonstrate financial commitment to the organization's long-term success.

Unidentified Influencers

As I spent time interacting with the leadership team of the business and in the organization, I began to identify the previously "unidentified influencers" (UIs) of the business. My first interaction with Zack on the night shift impressed me because of his knowledge of the technical aspects of the business, his experience in the business, and his keen sense of what was good and what could be improved within the culture. Zack was also actively involved in the business's safety team and his peers demonstrated and communicated respect for him in many ways, including their body language when he was present. Conversely, as I interacted with some managers in the business, Zack's name was discussed with some level of frustration. Frustration by managers about specific employees can be valid and warranted;

however, I've experienced the vast majority of the "frustrating employee" with significant tenure as a result of the manager being pushed and challenged by the employee. With Zack, it was clear to me that he clearly felt ownership of the business, but he was frustrated by the lack of follow through and follow up on key issues and opportunities he saw in the operation.

In another path of discovering who the UIs in the business were, I was sought out by a team on one of the night shifts (the organization operated 24 hours a day, seven days a week with four shifts that worked 12-hour days/nights, three to four days a week with a week break every other month). This team came up to me after my first, introductory town hall to challenge one of my keystone introductory points: I always ask for "a show of hands of the individuals who planned to come to work that day and make errors, create deviations, or cause an accident." Of course, no one raises their hand, but the point allows the room to lighten up and for me to accentuate the point that people don't come to work to fail or make errors. This team asked me to come in on one of the nights they were scheduled to work. They wanted to show me the path of a significant error that had been made on their shift, which had resulted in two of the operators receiving a disciplinary warning because of the negative impact on the batch of product (each batch manufactured at the site had significant financial value, as well as importance for supply of medicine by our clients to their patients). Right there, as the town hall meeting was over, I asked them if we could go through the scenario right now. They agreed, and asked for 30 minutes to gather the documents they wanted to go through with me.

As we gathered in the conference room a half hour later, the table was filled with the significant documentation associated with a batch produced for a biological drug substance. They had three specific portions of the batch record marked, and they asked me to read the first one. As I read the instructions of the batch record followed for a specific part of the process, I had many questions as I went through it to check for understanding. After I finished reading this section of the batch record, I was directed to a specific instruction and asked what actions I would take to adhere to the instruction. After confessing my lack of direct hands-on experience in biologics drug substance manufacturing, I provided what I ascertained as the logical actions I would take in accordance with the instruction. The team reacted with laughter and a few comments of sarcasm. I knew I had been set up, and now the moment they wanted to stage for me was upon us.

The spokesperson of the team stated, "And you would be written up for causing a deviation that negatively impacted the batch!" The other portions of the batch record that were marked were also part of the deviation because this "operator error" led to the next two errors, as they are consequential to the first decision. The spokesperson then remarked, "You were right in the Town Hall meeting — we don't come to work to create errors, but the tools we have to work with *create* those errors! We've been telling our supervisor and manager that we need input to the batch-record writing process to provide the operative view. We've been told our input is not valid because the technical writers in the technical services group have more experience and capability, and the clients sign off on the batch records.[1] We have asked for the opportunity to perform 'dry runs' with the batch records before we activate them live, like we used to in the past. Unfortunately, batch records are finalized at the last minute, and management won't take an extra shift to ensure the batch records are right the first time. The lack of input from operations leads to these errors frequently. The result, operators are written up for mis-reading or not interpreting vague instructions properly!"

---

1 Remember the disconnect of the organization referred to in the beginning of this story? This situation was exhibit A.

I asked the team to give me a few days to investigate several things:

1. What mechanisms could be put into place to review batch records before they are executed?

2. How could we improve the batch record instructions to remove vague and unclear steps?

3. Are there any other specific facts that resulted in the disciplinary action being taken that the team might not have shared with me?

The team agreed with this timing, as this night was their last one for the week. I told them I would get back to them the following week. As I walked away from the team and reflected upon the day and this situation, I was excited! I knew, from past experience that a few of the team members were hopeful that I would follow up with them as promised. I also knew there were others on the team that were setting themselves up for another "I told you so" moment, if I failed to follow through on my commitment to them. I knew this moment would be one of the first examples of positive change and reconnecting the organizational silos that had evolved. I couldn't wait to get going!

Organizational Relics

It might be archaic to do so, but my first assessment of a new facility and organization is always a tour of the restrooms, locker rooms, and gowning rooms of the business. I'm not interested in the ones that visitors or clients use, but the ones that the employees use every day. These areas can provide the first insight into whether or not there is a true commitment by the organization to operate and care for the business at a high level. Overall, considering that I'd just joined on to lead a highly regulated site, I expected the superficial appearance to be good, which it was. Unfortunately, looking inside of some of the lockers, I saw violations of Good Manufacturing Practices (GMP), work shoes stored with white residue on them, and coveralls that were neatly stacked but all XXL and Medium coveralls were missing. I saw clear signs of lack of attention and care to the small details, which piqued my senses in walking around the operation.

As I walked further into the operation, I had in mind from my experience (and from reading the business's Standard Operating Procedure [SOP] what to expect to see in the adherence to gowning practices to protect the product and the operation. Additionally, I was interested in seeing how well the organization adhered to the use of Personal Protective Equipment (PPE). Both GMP gowning and PPE use are signs of not only the commitment and engagement of management, but also a signal of the environment of ownership embedded in the culture. As I walked around, fully gowned in the coveralls, shoe covers, hair net, and beard covering, my senses were on full alert (visual, sounds, and smells). My first encounter was with an operator whose coveralls were not fully zipped up, exposing undergarments they wore to work, which should have been totally covered in a GMP environment. I saw men with beards whose beard covers were pulled down on their chins and not covering all their facial hair. I saw a couple of women who had skipped the vital mirror-check to ensure all their hair was tucked under their hair cover. All these signs pointed to the organization's comfort with "going through the motions," and the lack of development of the culture required to manufacture very serious biologic drug substances. I was pleased to see consistent use of safety glasses and hearing protection; however, one operator was performing a task that required a face shield, but he wore only safety glasses. The lack of use of handrails when climbing and descending stairs was a risk for injury (slipping down stairs is one of the top causes of injury in manufacturing operations), and the site had significant stairways to platforms throughout the operation.

Both GMP gowning and PPE use are signs of not only the commitment and engagement of management, but also a signal of the environment of ownership embedded in the culture.

When I'm in observation mode, walking around the operational area, I pay attention to the postings on the walls. I'm drawn to items such as graphs, meeting notes, announcements, and messages to see if they are up-to-date as well as to learn something about the culture by making note of the content/focus of the postings. A consistent theme at this particular organization was that the postings were out of date, but at some point, they were relevant and posted with purpose. Beyond the lack of follow-up and feedback indicated by the postings, room operational labels were mostly current to the status of the room. Unfortunately, as a regulatory requirement, room labels must be current and descriptive of the current task being performed; and I noted some rooms with labels that were not current.

For effectiveness in the introduction of change, positive and good practices are also something I seek. One of the first bright spots of touring around was the overall housekeeping and cleanliness. The facility was designed, constructed, and outfitted for the purpose of its intended use. The equipment and spare parts were appropriately stored and labelled. Behaviorally, I was glad to be approached by three different operators, who didn't recognize me, nor associate the Site Director as being someone who would be walking around on a Sunday afternoon. These interactions were outstanding, and the people who challenged me as someone they didn't know led to very productive conversations. Interestingly, after the third interaction, I came across a supervisor for the first time during my two hours of walking around (not a good sign). Encouragingly, I observed a change-over taking place on a piece of equipment by three operators. I was very impressed with their referring to the SOP, the three-way communication (instruction, repeat, verify), so the foundations were in place for adhering to procedures and working together in a safe manner.

Summarizing the analysis, I was encouraged about the opportunity to engage and re-engage the people in the organization. The evidence I found during my "organizational archeological dig" proved some effective ways of working and very good past initiatives had been introduced. The challenge would be in re-engaging those who had bought into past initiatives, while engaging those who hadn't bought in or were never invited to participate. People don't lose their sense of "here we go again" with new initiatives, particularly after they've experienced the apathy of leadership's lack of engagement or follow up. Ahead was the rewarding task of re-engaging, shaping, and changing the culture one piece at a time; specifically employing a "pull from the organization" rather than a "push from leadership." A key step I would need to take was a rigorous assessment of the managers who I inherited with my new role. I would need to act quickly to identify managers who were responsible for not following up and being consistent in leading day-to-day operations properly, as well as not following through on past initiatives. After identifying which managers weren't delivering, I needed to assess whether they could be an asset to the work ahead or a barrier to success. Ultimately, some individuals' roles would change to meet the needs of the business and organization. The changes to be made would be dependent upon each person's willingness to commit themselves to championing the future changes." In short, we would provide hope of a new day to those who seek it and then employ them as change agents for the work ahead! Other key steps to take included, re-engaging with the night shift team who took time to share their issues with me, and engaging other champions to change the culture.

People don't lose their sense of "here we go again" with new initiatives, particularly after they've experienced the apathy of leadership's lack of engagement or follow up.

The "Journey to Excellence" began shortly after the cultural diagnosis phase was complete. The diagnosis steps I've shared with you in this story can be used by you! Whether you're joining a new business, taking on a new role, or you desire to evaluate your current culture with fresh eyes, consider using the steps I've outlined in this story and the lessons outlined below. They have worked for me many times, and they will for you too!

 LESSONS LEARNED

1. To influence a change, a leader must invest time to understand the current state of the business and culture before communicating future changes. You will have to be a listener and an observer, and seek validation of views formed before articulating your assessment.

2. A leader who needs to initiate a change must earn the right to do so and to be listened to by the organization. Again, you've been hired as a boss, and the people will award you with the label of a leader (or not) based on your behaviors, actions, and decisions.

3. Seek and find leaders and unidentified influencers of the organization and validate their standing amongst the people of the organization through diligence of point #1 above.

4. At the right time, communicate what you've found in an inquisitive, non-accusatory manner. Seek to understand, not to embarrass or call out.

5. Be prepared to make quicker changes with more senior-level employees, specifically those who don't recognize the validity of issues most of the organization sees. What I'm talking about are issues that others talk and laugh about (openly or in small groups) in a sad and sarcastic manner — those are the issues that many senior-level employees are blind to, but the "I told you so" people in your organization use as tools.

6. Successful cultural transformations are embedded when the people pull the changes into their teams rather than having those changes forced upon them or pushed by bosses. Recognition of the impact of culture on the success of individuals, teams, and the business must occur within key influencers of the organization.

THE MIRROR TEST

Questions for Self-Reflection

1. Has anyone in your workplace lit a fire in your heart regarding the job you are doing? How good did this make you feel? How can you pay this forward to one of your fellow employees?

2. If you believe in an initiative, keep the fire going! How can you maintain momentum, even if your superiors lose focus on what motivates you? In my experience, team members who "pick up the ball" and run with it on their own demonstrate commitment and initiative. People do pay attention!

3. Think about the unidentified influencers in your organization or team. Why are they influential? Do they positively influence

or detract from the positive direction? How can you learn from them, and develop yourself to become a positive influencer?

CHAPTER 9

People Are the Solution, Not the Problem

Regardless of what stage of your career you currently find yourself in (or your title or role in an organization), if you're like most people, **you want to be valued and be relevant**. The rise of social media usage has served to highlight this universal desire. Online, we present and share messages, likes or dislikes or other reactions, endless selfies, strong opinions, and usually our most appealing attributes to increase our following and popularity. But long before Facebook or Instagram, we all wanted to be accepted, valued, relevant, and liked. The difference between today and yesterday is the speed, timing, and reach that feedback (whether it's being given or received) achieves. Our current ability to exchange information has evolved (or devolved, depending on your view!) in remarkable ways.

What is true in our personal lives is also true in business. In every organization, people want to be relevant and contribute to the success of the team. Relevance comes in many different shapes and sizes, and the term is subjectively defined by each of us. Throughout my working career, I've made it my goal to know all of my co-workers' names and something about them (which also helps in remembering their names). This practice can be challenging when you're responsible for an organization of 1,000+ employees, but the goal can be accomplished through a bit of effort and by practicing "management by walking around" — a concept made popular by performance improvement guru Tom Peters. I've adapted his terminology with a twist, called "*leadership* by walking around."

Relevance comes in many different shapes and sizes, and the term is subjectively defined by each of us.

One of the most successful approaches I've employed has been spending time in the actual workplace to gain insights and to learn, first-hand, my team members' duties. The impact of a leader who genuinely seeks to understand someone's duties and responsibilities communicates to them that they are important and that their leader is interested in them. **Actions speak so much louder than words.**

Years ago, as an HR director, I made a habit of going into to the manufacturing site twice a month and working from 9:00 p.m. to 3:00 a.m. My goals were clear:

1. Be available on a consistent basis for individuals who worked on night shifts

2. Get to know the individuals who work on night shift

3. Gain insights into our opportunities for improving the organization's performance.

This investment of spending time with the people on the front line — those who typically received less attention from leadership in general — was beneficial in accomplishing all the goals listed above. In addition, as a leader in the business, I learned more about what worked well and what didn't work well, and employees drew comfort in being noticed by someone higher up the corporate ladder, which ultimately helped them build a sense of trust in me.

One night, I was in a granulation suite. Granulation is the process in which active ingredients and excipients (i.e., non-active ingredients formulated with the active ingredient of a drug) are blended before being compressed into tablets or filled into capsules. I was working with two people who were granulating (or blending) a batch of product. As they worked, and as I mostly watched and asked questions, it was obvious to them that I had a specific interest in their work on this process. Engaging in this manner evolved into a discussion regarding two significant quality problems that were under investigation on batches previously manufactured in this production area. As these workers performed the night's duties and the process was being executed, I probed more deeply in discussion with the operators regarding recent quality issues.

Very quickly, they identified some probable root causes for the quality deviations, one of which was a compression issue in the next step of the process. They showed me the inconsistencies in the batch record. The inconsistencies resulted from vague instructions that opened the steps in the process to the interpretation of each individual, creating error traps. It later turned out the variations that drove the deviation were directly linked to this area of the process!

Another interesting insight I gained from observing the operators make the batch was that a particular step taken to load chemicals into the batch was physically demanding on the operators. It required operators to partner in lifting multiple 50-kg drums of material to discharge the contents into the blend. This process step created two error traps. First, it was physically difficult and had already resulted in two work-related injuries for back strains. Second, the friction caused between the stainless-steel mixing vessel and the fiber drum being discharged introduced fibers into the blend, causing a quality defect.

I asked the operators for any alternatives they had thought about to eliminate the requirement for operators having to manually manipulate the drums. It turns out they had discussed this previously and had drawn up rough sketches of a drum lift with a vibrating mechanism, which would be ideal to use in this part of the process. I asked them who they had shared their idea with, and they said they hadn't shared it. Curious now, I asked them why they had gone to the effort of designing a solution and not shared it with engineering or even their supervisor. They replied in unison, "We never see engineering, and our supervisor isn't really interested in our ideas!"

"Wow" was what I wanted to say, but I told them I would take their design and follow up on any opportunities we had available or could pursue. Over the next couple of months, engineering adjusted schedules to work on night shifts and engage with operators. I also took the opportunity to begin coaching and mentoring the supervisor and the manager of the area, which evolved into a regular forum of all supervisors on each shift coming together to share ideas about how to engage with their operators in their own respective departments and how to cross-train across departments.

The ultimate result was a win for the business with improved results in safety, quality, and efficiency. And, in large measure, it was driven by employees realizing that they are relevant. The key action of engaging and following through communicates how important all employees are to the organization and to the business's success. Of course, there was no way I would let this successful situation go unshared with the entire organization. With the collaboration between the operators, engineers, and supervisors, the new vibratory-enabled drum lifts were designed, built, and installed (and many other steps necessary to make a process change in an FDA-regulated business, like validation, testing, etc.). In the subsequent Town Hall meetings with the entire organization, I was able to share the story and success of these two operators' idea! I had two objectives to sharing this meaningful story:

1. To ensure recognition of the idea from these two individuals was celebrated, along with the team members who collaborated on bringing the idea into reality!

2. Through sharing the story, others in the organization get to hear, see, and know the ideas they have thought about will be followed through on.

We were overwhelmed with ideas that came forward, as the experts (those who perform tasks every day) believed and trusted their input was both valued and acted upon. As a side note to the recognition, a grassroots team was formed to focus simply on recognition of ideas generated and implemented. The main hallway in the site soon became a place where ideas and originators were posted for all to see; the Wall of Fame was established!

Sometimes, the Only Way Up is Out

Through my career, I've encountered more than one situation where I've felt myself relegated to irrelevance. The most marked situation was following the acquisition of our business by a new company. I was highly engaged with the current company, and I led the due diligence and assessment of the acquiring company's European sites. Throughout the deal closing period and during integration following the close, I was highly engaged with the new leadership and the planning and delivery of communications for the business I led, which was twice the size of any other site in the combined businesses.

As the integration of our organizations proceeded, new leadership delivered its own expectations. Leadership teams were being formed, and the process of getting to know each other was running at full steam. As I got to know the new leadership and they were getting to know me, it was hard to ignore our differences in styles and approaches to leading the business. Over the course of the next several weeks, the differences escalated to impassioned discussions and I allowed "some lines to be drawn in the sand."

One of these proverbial lines was based on an inconsistency between the significant efforts to drive down unessential costs from the business (which the organization was doing successfully and with enthusiasm), versus an insistence to add additional costs of employing new senior-level people to the leadership team (new positions, higher costs). In short, the inconsistency of actions and decisions (i.e., reducing costs on the shop floor, while increasing costs at the leadership level) would send an incongruent message to the people.

Another key point of difference centered on the costs and investments necessary to sustain the compliance profile of the business I led under the requirements of the FDA. The FDA sets expectations for expertise of the staff, maintenance and calibration of equipment, and consistency of the processes executed to manufacture drugs. A requirement to cross the threshold of below minimal standards of compliance to FDA regulations to achieve lower costs was short-term thinking and potentially damaging to the business. For the three months following, I was excluded from meetings, sessions were scheduled with members of my staff without my knowledge, and my team was receiving directions that shifted priorities away from the delivery of our product and service to our clients.

When I requested meetings to discuss ways of working, communications, and even monthly results that were exceeding targets, I received no response. The dynamic of being relegated into irrelevance was difficult for my team, who I had led through a significant transformation across all aspects of our business during the past two years. The situation for me became clear, and I recognized my future of leading this organization was going to be short lived. I coached my team to align with the new leadership, while grasping the reality of my ultimate departure, something I kept confidential from colleagues — a reality my wife and I only entertained in private for quite some time.

As I lived through this experience, I viewed it as a positive development for me and my future, because it was clear I could not be successful in the new organization. But it wasn't entirely easy. My team and I had built strong connections that went beyond work, and losing that day-to-day interaction was surely a loss for me professionally and personally. The situation was new to me, as I contemplated my pending departure from the leadership of this site. As much as I focused upon the positive (with Sandy encouraging me at every turn), the reality of being unemployed for the first time in my adult life was one I had to get my head around. Ultimately, Sandy and I were prepared for this pending change in my employment status, but the timing of the actual event to take place was unknown. I knew from my experience that my departure would have to align with the introduction of my replacement, so I predicted steps were being taken by the company to prepare for the change to come.

And then, a decision by my boss let me know the timing of the event! I asked my boss for permission to take off the Monday following the July 4th weekend. I was surprised by his rejection of my request, which was the first time I'd not been allowed to take a day of vacation. There was no business reason for the rejection, so I surmised that he had planned and lined up for that Monday to be my departure day. While still nervous about the future, I was comforted in a way to know the timeline.

Recognizing the situation for what it was, my wife and I cleaned out my office that Sunday, and I left my company-issued car in the parking lot. The next day, I was summoned to meet with my boss in a conference room at a local hotel. The meeting with my boss was short — less than two minutes. He left, and I sat with his HR partner to go through the separation agreement. Even though the separation was difficult on some levels, I did appreciate the company's treatment of me in the agreement. I walked away from the meeting with a mixture of feelings and emotions. The uncertainty of the future was intimidating, while the feeling of freedom was exhilarating. Sandy and I looked ahead and focused on the excitement of the future and what life had in store for us! This change opened up wonderful new opportunities for us both, and we were blessed by the path ahead of us. Ultimately, I was only irrelevant in the eyes of those whose view doesn't match my own.

The uncertainty of the future was intimidating, while the feeling of freedom was exhilarating.

 LESSONS LEARNED

1. Some leaders look at their people as a problem, while successful leaders view people as the solution!

2. The ideas on how to improve a business are known by the individuals who perform the work on a day-in and day-out basis. To unlock those ideas, people need to be valued as relevant, and be confident their ideas will be received and evaluated.

3. If you want to communicate to someone that they are important, go to them in their work area, listen to them with genuine interest, and then follow up. The first two actions reinforce and validate the third, which communicates "You are important to me."

4. There are some individuals in supervisory roles or even functional roles of expertise (e.g., engineers or accountants) who

don't yet know how to engage and interact with people effectively. Coaching, sharing, and setting a positive example for them to follow helps build their confidence and comfort in interacting and engaging with people in all parts of the company.

5. Never define people by their job or title! What's inside a person defines who they are, not their job, so everyone should be treated with respect, worthy of your time as a leader. Create experiences that inspire, motivate, and develop a sense of ownership!

6. We should be open to feedback from others, but we must not empower others to determine our relevance.

THE MIRROR TEST

Questions for Self-Reflection

1. What actions can you take to prevent an individual on your team from being relegated to an irrelevant status?

2. What will you do if you discover you are no longer aligned with the values or ways of working within your team or organization?

3. Do you have an idea you would like to discuss at work with your leadership? If so, what or who is stopping you? Find someone you trust who is in a leadership role, and present your idea to them.

CHAPTER 10

Speak from Your Heart

Leadership is perhaps never more important as it is during a crisis. At one of the businesses I led, we experienced a near-fatal accident that affected me deeply and taught me much. An employee had fallen from a one-person, motorized scaffold, suffering trauma from the fall and a severe laceration to his neck. I immediately was overwhelmed by an internal feeling — borne of my emotions and prior situations — that triggered actual physical manifestations. My skin felt charged with electricity, my thoughts were racing through my brain, and I could feel the adrenaline of fear course through my veins. From experience, I recognized that I needed a few moments to resolve this wash of my own feelings in order to allow my analytical self to take over my actions and set aside the emotions that had taken me over.

As I began the necessary interactions with my team — gain information on the health of the employee who fell, to assess the emotional health and feelings of each person on my team, the impact on people in my business, and the impact on the business itself — I used three areas of assessment as priorities:

> **Priority #1:** Secure the area of the accident for the investigation.

> **Priority #2:** Ensure my HR team was on the scene and interacting with the employees to calm and comfort them with the little information we had.

Priority #3: Get to the emergency room to be with the family members who had just received news of the accident and were arriving at the hospital, panicked and scared.

After I had been in the waiting room with the family for about an hour, the doctor came out to provide an update. The family asked me to stay with them while the doctor covered the condition of their loved one. Fortunately, the report was the best news that could have been delivered. The employee had significant contusions on his shoulder and side from the impact with the floor. The laceration of his neck, which caused significant blood loss, had missed the jugular vein, just narrowly. The diagnosis was that, over time, he would make a full recovery. As we hugged and cried and prayed together, the family expressed their appreciation for my being there with them. They told me they would be okay, and I assured them I would stay in touch with them.

Driving back to my plant from the hospital, I gained clarity on the different courses of action that needed to take place. My superiors in the company needed to be informed and know the individual was going to recover. The investigation had to be conducted quickly, but thoroughly. Most importantly, the organization I led had to be informed, which requires some context. The business expanded across a 600-acre campus with more than a million square feet of building space populated by 1,300+ people across multiple shifts. The ability to communicate directly to the organization was challenging, but it was necessary.

By the end of the night, some key factors that contributed to the accident were identified by the investigation team. John was an employee of a construction firm that worked in partnership with my business. He had taken the initiative to install a 4-foot by 8-foot piece of metal onto an opening in the ceiling of an area that was being refurbished — taking on this task without performing a risk assessment or following the procedure for gaining the proper permits required to perform working at heights (a requirement for any task being performed above 3 feet in our business).

Further, the injured person had used the wrong tool because it was already in the room and was easier than going to get the right one. And he had performed the task without anyone else in the area. In the end, there were more than two dozen factors identified that contributed to this near-fatal accident. All of them would be addressed, but the most challenging was the prevailing culture that allowed this type of risky behavior in the first place.

I knew it was vital to send a strong message regarding safety, to find ways to motivate employees and contractors to follow procedures designed for everyone's safety, and to change the culture that enabled this behavior. The path forward to deliver this message was challenging; however, the need to personally address the situation was without question.

To accommodate most of the organization as quickly as possible, we cleared out the large warehouse for up to 800 people to participate in a standing meeting. We quickly adjusted operational schedules to ensure most of the people on day and night shifts could come together by overlapping their schedules for the meeting, in addition to scheduling additional meetings to ensure every individual ultimately received the same message within 48 hours of the accident.

As the large workforce gathered, the noise of conversations and movement filled the warehouse. This mandatory meeting was the first of its kind, and we did not circulate a topic or agenda in advance. I had arranged for a two-person lift (i.e., cherry picker) to be in place, so I could be both heard and seen from an elevated position. Important to me and the message was my ability to look directly into the eyes of as many of the employees as I could focus on while speaking. At the meeting start time, I asked for everyone to settle down and give me their full attention.

I told the employees about the near-fatal accident that had taken place. I shared with them — without guarding my emotions — my drive to the hospital, facing the uncertainty of whether John would live. I shared with them an insight into the physical reaction I felt, just as I'd felt years ago when Barbara was struck by lightning and killed in one of my previous businesses

My objective was to bring everyone to the understanding and the feeling of losing, or nearly losing, a life in our place of business. The non-verbal body language of the employees and the facial expressions of those in the audience clearly demonstrated that their attention was fully focused on the message being delivered.

My remarks then moved to my second objective, which was to take this tragedy and mark it as a time to change how we would work going forward, what we would focus on, and how we would collectively hold ourselves accountable for our own safety and the safety of our colleagues. I closed the meeting with an absolute mandate regarding our attention and strict adherence to the procedures in place to protect ourselves and our business.

I re-enforced the message with the following comment: "Everyone in this warehouse is special, unique, and critical for our business to be successful. But I have to be absolutely clear: If there are any individuals in this warehouse who do not believe this message applies to them or who don't believe they can hold themselves and others accountable for safety, I ask you to speak to your supervisor about resignation. No one will look to those who might resign as bad people ... just not a fit for our organization. Safety matters."

I closed the meeting and descended from the platform to mingle with the employees. There was a lot of discussion taking place among groups that seemed to form naturally. As I mingled and eaves-dropped, I heard a lot of validation regarding the message I had delivered. Several groups pulled me into their discussions to ask questions about the accident and how John was doing. The dominant feedback I heard for several weeks following the meeting was a sincere appreciation for the opportunity to come together, all at once, to hear a strong but necessary message.

More importantly, the actions taken after that meeting were evident in a significant improvement in safety and the interactions among individuals that I witnessed taking place across the campus. Crisis had made us stronger ... and safer.

 ## LESSONS LEARNED

1. An organization, which functions as a collective living being, sometimes needs the norm to be disrupted to make a point extremely clear and to establish focus. The key is to employ this mechanism rarely, lest it becomes the norm.

2. As a leader, you must consciously assess moments or situations as tools to affect a needed change, and use it to improve the organization.

3. There are a few areas of focus that leaders can employ to bring an organization together and focus on business goals. A strong emphasis on the health, safety, and the well-being of everyone should be something everyone can understand and get behind.

4. Leaders in an organization must develop feedback skills, learning how to give focused counsel to employees.

5. The organization must hear from the leader's heart, not just their head.

THE MIRROR TEST

Questions for Self-Reflection

1. Are you witnessing something in your workplace that could be potentially harmful to someone? Please share your observation with your leadership. You may save a life!

2. Procedures and policies are in place for a reason, but they do become irrelevant over time. Think about your business ... Are there procedures everyone ignores because they know they no longer are applicable? How do you prevent this "slippery slope" from invalidating the critical procedures and policies from the ones that are no longer important?

CHAPTER 11

Trust, But Verify

In 2012, following a business Town Hall in which we discussed the safety of our workforce and the accountability of our staff to ensure safe ways of working, I was approached by a group of employees. This was the norm. Following the robust Q & A sessions held at the end of the Town Halls, I generally would be sought by folks who were more comfortable asking questions in a less public fashion. The "side conversation" is often where the magic happened and I got the opportunity to hear what people were thinking.

In this instance, a group of eight employees gathered around me, and the leader of the group said he wanted to ask me a question on behalf of the group. I said sure, because I appreciated these interactions. The group leader said, "Carson, you just communicated to the entire workforce the priority you place on the safety of your employees, correct?"

Given my years of experience, I immediately suspected the question was a set-up by the group. I confidently answered affirmatively as I scanned the others for their reaction to my response. The leader followed up with the question, or rather a challenge, that he wanted to raise in front of the group. He said, "Well then, how can you expect individuals to be focused on working safely when we are required to work seven days a week for two months in a row without a break? We can't maintain a safety focus with that kind of work schedule because we're humans, not machines."

My radar was on point. This gathering and the questions were both a set-up and an ambush, but I know there are always some valid points raised during these interactions. Leaders, over time, should develop a sense of when to challenge a situation rather than leave it alone. In this encounter, I'd been leading businesses for more than 15 years, so my radar was well-tuned.

As the group leader and his team stared at me and waited for my response, I told them that I understood their concern. Working seven days a week without a day off would be an onerous schedule. I told them that, in our industry, there would be times (such as during medicine shortages) that might demand some extreme work schedules. I reminded them about when the flu epidemic was plaguing the U.S. and we had to work some exceedingly long schedules to ensure vaccinations were available to the public. I further reminded them that, even in this extreme example, we were able to re-shape the shift structures and employ additional people to reduce the workload after the first month.

I then committed to the group that I would investigate their question and get back to them with a response.

I knew instinctively that their assertion and complaint was probably exaggerated or lacked context. Odds are, you too have experienced a story or situation with questionable facts. And most of us have been told a story and accepted the "facts" on face value, only to regret it later.

In our current age of Google, social media hoaxes, and information suddenly being labelled "fake news," we have become more inclined to fact check stories we hear outside work. But, how about inside work?

Over my years, I've experienced factual and fictional stories presented to me by individuals at all different organizational levels. Being someone who trusts until trust has been broken, I've had to focus consciously on determining when stories require a fact-checking investigation. And, to be upfront with you, I don't always get it right!

That afternoon, I took a list of the eight employees' names and asked HR to run an overtime report for each of them. When I received the report later in the day, it showed that only one individual on that team had worked a Saturday shift. Further, two of the employees had just returned the week before from five days of vacation — all of this just before they challenged me about their work schedule.

This was a classic example of not letting facts get in the way of a good story or never passing up the opportunity to ambush the leader and grandstand for a moment. The following day, I went out into the area where the team worked, and I found the group leader. We went to a conference room for a talk. I reiterated to him that my commitment to the safety of our workforce indeed was the highest priority, and I had followed up on the question he asked me in front of his team.

I saw him shifting nervously as I shared with him the work schedules of his crew over the past two months. As he looked at the report, I said that I now had a question for him, "I want to understand your team's motivation for the situation that you initiated yesterday." The group leader hesitated, and I could tell he was caught off guard by my follow up.

After a full two minutes during which I sat silently waiting for a response, he put down the papers and confirmed that his team had not been working seven days a week for two months but said the department head had talked about the *potential* that such a schedule might be required. Again, I let silence fill the room for an uncomfortable moment. I then looked the group leader in the eye and asked him, "What is the true point you attempted to make by ambushing me with your team after the meeting?"

He said, "Summer is coming, and we don't want to be tied up every weekend with work."

I asked him if he had discussed this with his supervisor or the head of the department. He told me they had held a meeting that day, and that a schedule had been worked out for a rotation of weekend work among the four crews over the coming months. He said his crew would have to work only one weekend per month to fulfill our client's need for product.

I told him I appreciated his sharing this with me, but I wanted to give him some feedback. I know he was thinking, "Here it comes!" I told him that I had looked through his background and noted that he had been a great employee for us, even being promoted to a group leader role earlier in the year. As he accepted the responsibilities of the group leader position, he had also accepted the accountability for his team, as well as the business's success. I told him I was disappointed in his making the decision to grandstand with me in front of his team, and that I could tell from his work history this behavior was not typical.

He acknowledged that he had let his team put him up to challenging me in front of them. I asked him if he had learned anything from this situation, and what change he would make in similar situations in the future. He said, "First, I've learned that you follow through on your commitments as a leader and you investigate the background of a situation. I see how important following up and investigating situations are." He next told me that, as a group leader, he had the responsibility to employ the proper channels within our organization to address issues and seek help.

I agreed with him on his "lessons learned" and I closed the conversation by telling him that we all make mistakes or err in our judgement. What separates those who succeed from those who go down the wrong path are the changes we make when we encounter mistakes. I told him that I still thought favorably of him and told him my door was always open ... to call upon me if he encountered future situations that he wasn't sure how to handle. Over the next two years, this group leader became a champion of change and continuous improvement in our business; and we continued to have periodic one-on-ones with the primary focus on his development.

 LESSONS LEARNED

1. Every individual can get caught in a difficult situation by others. When that happens, it's important to listen intently to what is being said. But it's just as important to do some fact-finding of your own.

2. It's critical to follow up with those who ask questions or make claims, to let them know they are important to you.

3. Individuals who put themselves into awkward situations should be given the opportunity to learn from those moments and adjust their future actions accordingly. How many times you should offer such opportunities truly depends on the specific positive and negative contributions the individual delivers to the organization. If the negatives far outweigh the positives, fewer opportunities are warranted, and vice versa.

THE MIRROR TEST

Questions for Self-Reflection

1. Have you encountered people at your workplace who say or portray things in a dishonest way? Everyone has observed (or will eventually observe) this in their work area. What will you do when this happens? How can you prepare yourself for this uncomfortable situation?

2. It's easy to get caught up in the moment with your team, giving in to group-think or allying yourself with others whose words or behaviors are less than virtuous. Upon reflection, what can you do to prevent yourself or your team from getting caught up in a moment that might negatively impact your reputation at work?

3. When you've been challenged or cornered at work, have you asked for time to reflect and gather facts before responding?

CHAPTER 12

Inspirational Leadership Is Found at All Levels

One of my early life experiences in leadership and influencing a culture was during my freshman year at Wake Forest University.

Being young, naïve, in love with football, and passionate about my team, I was as prepared as I could be to enter into the world of college athletics. The insights I gained during my playing days have become clearer over the years, as I have reflected on this wonderful experience and reminisced with former coaches and teammates. I've carried with me so many positive experiences from my time as a member of Wake Forest's football team that have contributed to who I am today.

I recognize the blessings of having the ability to participate in athletics at the collegiate level. Admittedly, I grasped the opportunity to be a part of the 1979 Demon Deacons football team with a chip on my shoulder, motivated by a need to define myself. I was invited to walk on as a freshman in order to be a part of the team. Not receiving the recognition of an athletic scholarship drove me to prepare diligently before summer practice began, just as I had since my experience in the seventh grade (when I was cut from the roster of the school basketball team when the final team was named).

The summer before I was to arrive on campus at Wake Forest,
I committed myself to being in peak condition. I also needed to
earn money, so I needed to find a job and a schedule that would
accommodate both of my needs, earning money and building up
my strength, agility, and stamina. A father of one of my high school
classmates owned and operated a farm in our community. John,
the farmer, had played football at NC State and he went on to play
professional football in Canada. John understood what I wanted to
accomplish in the summer and he guaranteed me that working on
his farm in the summer would get me into great shape and ensure
I was acclimated to the heat of summer that I would face when
I arrived at Wake. In addition to working on the farm that summer,
I spent countless hours lifting weights, running sprints, and running
long distances after I got off work. I followed the pre-season workout
regimen that was sent to all players — and did even more. I was set
to make my mark on the team as someone who was fully committed,
despite my perception that the team was not fully committed to me
because they didn't offer me a scholarship.

My first day with the team, as 33 freshmen gathered in the dorm, was
eye opening. I knew I was undersized just by viewing the large guys
in the room. It was a bit intimidating. In fact, my mom (who delivered
me to school) shared her concern for my well-being as she saw the
size of the men who I would be playing with in college.

The freshmen were drilled beyond exhaustion for a week before the
upperclassmen were scheduled to report to summer camp. I was
well prepared, although the coaches apparently had designed these
initial seven days to inflict an intense level of bodily soreness through
diabolically designed drills. Somehow, we all were able to crawl
to our dorm rooms at night and recover enough for the following
day's torture. My dorm room was on the 4th floor, and climbing those
stairs took significant effort after the hours upon hours of drills the
coaches ran us through.

Later in the season, upon reflection, I recognized the goal of the coaches was to fully orient the freshmen on the expectations of our new lives as members of the team. While each member of the freshman group had been leaders and stellar players in high school, we all quickly learned our place as new members of a team of men. After a week, the upperclassmen joined the freshmen, and I felt I had physically shrunk as I took in the gathering of men who joined us. I was no longer playing with boys!

Looking back, I realized that's when some key experiences in leadership took place. I'll always think back fondly upon one of our team's captains. (Our team captains played a special role in my life back then. One of them, Bert, moved into my dorm room for a few weeks, until the house he'd rented off campus was ready to be moved into with some other players; James went on to be enshrined in the Atlantic Coast Conference Hall of Fame; and Syd, who was an exceptional player, went on to have a good career in the NFL.) I can go on talking about my fellow teammates, but you'll probably get bored. So let me share a foundational memory about one of these guys, which left an impression just as the season was kicking off. Sarge, who managed all the equipment for the team, was issuing our gear for the season and before we started full contact. James and I happened to collect our gear at the same time and headed to the locker room to stow it away and dress for the first team practice.

As we walked to the locker room, Sarge yelled at me to make sure I found the locker with my name on it, given that the lockers had been permanently assigned. I'll spare you the precise nature of Sarge's language and temperament. James told me just to follow him and to ignore Sarge and his colorful language, who apparently genuinely wanted the best for his players. James shared that Sarge had a great heart, but he also played his role in breaking down our individualism to become fully invested as team members.

We walked together down the rows of lockers, and James told me my locker should be beside my teammate JK's because our jersey numbers were in numerical sequence with each other. We walked down the row and found JK's locker, but the #86 locker had been skipped. Curious now, James and I continued to search for a locker with my name and number on it. We got to the last row of lockers, and there were three lockers on which white ankle tape had been placed. On the white tape at the top of these three lockers, names were written with a black marker.

James looked at me and said, "I'll check into what has happened here. All players are to have had the nice name plates engraved with your name and number to mark your locker." I recognized what had taken place and told James, "Don't worry about it. These lockers are for me, Mike, and Alan. We are the three walk-ons this year. I guess there wasn't consideration ahead of time regarding numbers for the walk-ons, or the coaches may not have been sure we would even show up."

James just shook his head and mumbled as he walked away. As I was stowing my gear, I heard a banging noise across from me. I look up and there was James. He had gathered all his gear and was throwing it into the locker beside mine. He then took out a roll of tape and a marker and wrote his name and number on it. He looked at me and grinned with a wink and said, "There are no walk-ons on this team, just teammates" as he wrote my number on the white tape beside my name!

As a Team, Who Do We Want to Be?

Through the painfully glorious weeks of summer camp, the team sweated gallons, bruised, and bled as we went through two practices a day with playbook study and meals in between. Each morning, we were greeted by the ever-present smell of cured tobacco that covered Winston-Salem from the RJ Reynolds tobacco company that was a dominant presence in the town. The odor, along with the heat and humidity, were just part of the experience, along with grueling drill after drill. Every evening, we met with the coaches, who provided a critique of the day's performance and the challenges to overcome the next day. Day by day, the coaches had choreographed the schedule to form a group of individuals into a team of people who were connected and committed to the team's success. At the close of these nightly sessions, our head coach would give us a talk.

His messages and the way he delivered them inspired me tremendously. He delivered a few key messages that became part of the character of the team, specifically defining us rather than allowing the team's history or sports journalists to define us. One of these messages was, "NEVER, NEVER, NEVER GIVE UP" — a mantra that became an often-repeated statement of encouragement throughout the upcoming season. Historically, Wake Forest's football team was in the bottom of the standings and had won just a single game out of the 12 played during the previous season. Coming into the 1979 season, Wake was picked to finish last in the conference, again!

This season was the head coach's second and, being a former player at Wake Forest, he focused on instilling pride in us and a spirit of reliance upon each other as a team. One night, midway through the grueling summer practices, the team was exhausted both physically and mentally. That day, fights had broken out among team members during practice and coaches had been yelling and screaming at each other.

Coach obviously had recognized this day as a pivotal one in defining who our team would be this year. He talked through all the positive strengths and the talent on this year's team — talents and character we probably couldn't see in ourselves and certainly weren't looking to see in our state of exhaustion. He talked about the pride he had in us for how hard everyone had worked during the off-season and how prepared every person was when they arrived for summer camp. He said that we must decide that night, in that room, who this team would be this season ... not only as individuals, but as one single unit. He acknowledged the tensions and conflicts of the day, saying,

> "Today our energy, our enthusiasm, and our focus on making sure no one on this team fails took a huge dip. There is no one outside this room to blame for this. We only need to look around the room, and in the mirror, to see who is responsible for today's performance. No one outside of this room will define who we are. No one else will win or lose a game for us, or execute our assignments, or push us to be the best we can be!

> "Look at our schedule this season. We're playing a very difficult line-up against Georgia, Auburn, Pat Dye's East Carolina, and our conference is very strong with NC State and UNC coming off strong seasons. I look at this schedule, and I ask you to think about this season as an opportunity! And I ask all of you to answer the knock of opportunity when it comes calling!

> "Ask yourself when you get back to your dorm, *how will you answer opportunity when it knocks?* This season opportunity will come knocking for our team and for every player here. Whether you are a senior, pre-season All-ACC, or one of our freshmen, ask this question and answer for yourself, *WHAT WILL YOU DO WHEN OPPORTUNITY KNOCKS?"*

> "You've done what it took to get opportunity's attention, and now it is up to each one of us to answer the call that opportunity will bring. If you already have made the decision to greet the knock with all your heart and soul, stand with me now and let me *hear* you!"

The room erupted as everyone jumped to their feet yelling, whistling, fist-pumping, and high-fiving with the chant, "Demon Deacons" reverberating over and over through the room. Wow! I could have run through a brick wall, and I promised myself to not let this feeling leave me. Ever.

Always Acknowledge a Good Play

As soon as the summer practices ended and the students filled the campus with noise and activity, the team transitioned into the rhythm of the schedule we would follow for the season. Early morning breakfast checks to make sure we were awake and getting the calories we needed, classes, weightlifting between classes, medical treatments, and then the team practices in the afternoon. After every practice, we'd check in for suppers in our isolated dining area, then head off to our individual group meetings (linebackers, running backs, etc.). To close the days, we met with tutors and attended study halls to do our course work before heading back to the dorms for bed.

I continued to work hard and develop the techniques the coaches drilled into us during our position's group workouts, as each group of the team (line backers, running backs, etc.) had coaches who worked on specific techniques to the positions we played. I relished the learning from my position coach — Coach Fair — and the times we would perform drills against the running backs, offensive linemen, etc. Being a freshman, I was designated as a "scout team member." The offensive and defensive scout teams were coached to play the defense or offense of the week's upcoming opponent. The practice squads enable the first and second team offensive and defensive squads to practice our game plans against the team we would face on Saturday. Every day, my scout team colleagues and

I would play the upcoming opponent's defense against our first- and second-string offense.

One day, our defensive coordinator happened to be watching our scout team play against the first team offense. We were preparing to play the University of Georgia that weekend, so we had a big challenge to test the offense and get them ready for the Bulldogs. On one play that week, I broke free from a double-team block by the left tackle and tight end. As I was free in the backfield on a passing play, my instincts took over and I drove my body into our quarterback. *UH OH!* The QB was never to be touched for fear of injuring him in practice, so I broke that golden rule! I can honestly say that the tongue lashing I received from the head coach made me feel like running away and hiding. What was worse, I'd hurt our starting QB, Jay (who had really shined in our first game, and he was critical to our success). As a side note, Jay did recover and performed brilliantly against Georgia. He was named *Sports Illustrated's* player of the week, so my mistake ended up not hurting the team. (Back to the story of that day ... Thank you for indulging me!) After what felt like an eternity, the head coach stopped yelling at me, and I walked back to the scout team huddle with my head down. As I got to the huddle, our defensive coordinator leaned closely to me and said, "That was a heck of a play, and I couldn't have stopped before I hit Jay either! You just won a position on our travel team this week. We need a wedge buster, and you're our man!" Suddenly, I felt ecstatic! I made the travel team! What a shift from the dog house to Cloud 9!

After practice, as we were getting cleaned up for dinner, one of our team's captains came up to me. Syd was a large guy, intimidating, but he put his arm around my shoulder and told me "That was one heck of a play out there! I heard you're traveling with the team. You're going to travel with me. You will sit with me on the bus and on the plane, and I'm going to look after you!" I honestly didn't know what to say. Here is this huge man, who went on to play for the Packers and the Cowboys, taking time to not only recognize me, but to make me feel comfortable as one of the four freshman who had made the travel team. Throughout the season, Syd was always available to talk to me, mentor me, and even kicked me in the butt if he felt I needed additional inspiration. I still hear his words in my thoughts from time to time, "Carse, you can be awesome at this game, but you won't realize your potential unless you leave it all on the field!"

 LESSONS LEARNED

1. It's the big things and the little things that communicate to others their value to you.

2. Preparation allows you to answer the knock of opportunity when it comes.

3. Sometimes, people make mistakes, but their effort and commitment are more valuable than the impact of their mistakes!

4. Hear what leaders say but listen to their actions.

5. Years later, a former Wake Forest football teammate shared with me that I was an inspiration to him — and he was a starter and team leader. I asked him why he made this comment and he said, "You brought everything you had to our team, you left it all on the field both in practice and in games, and you always came back for more, even when you shouldn't have because of your injured shoulder." The lesson: Even when you don't believe anyone is paying attention, they are!

THE MIRROR TEST

Questions for Self-Reflection

1. Teamwork makes the team work, as they say. How can you be a better team player in your workplace, home life, and personal life?

2. Everyone has experienced the disorientation of that first day on the job! What actions can you take to help the new people on your team feel welcomed?

3. We have all encountered situations where one thing is said, but we see actions that contradict the words. How can you provide feedback in a positive manner to help eliminate the apparent conflict between words and actions?

CHAPTER 13

Facing Adversity Reveals the Leader

As a follow up to "Inspirational Leadership Is Found at All Levels," I must share one of the best — and worst — examples of what leaders should be for their organization.

At the end of my freshman season at Wake, we had gone undefeated through the first half of the season until losing a tight game with North Carolina State University in a mud bowl. We rebounded and were 8-1 with two regular season games remaining. We lost badly to Clemson University on a nationally televised game and headed to Williams Brice Stadium to play the University of South Carolina's Gamecocks for our last game of the season.

Being too young to recognize that something had occurred that fragmented the coaching staff, I nevertheless did feel a difference had taken over the attitude and the mood of the coaches. As with every organization, an unaligned leadership team will negatively impact the organization they lead. The day of the game, there appeared to be a strong disconnect among the coaches. Rumors circulated that some of the coaches had gone to a local establishment the night before the game and had been involved in an altercation. The team noted some facial bruises and lacerations, and one member of the staff kept his sunglasses on all day, even indoors.

We lost badly that day to the University of South Carolina, but we were surprised in our locker room at the end of the game to receive the invitation to play Louisiana State University in the Tangerine Bowl in December. This invitation quickly elevated the mood of the team back to the enthusiasm that had been in place for most of the season.

Despite losing our last two games by large margins, our season continued, and practices resumed as normal. The prospect of playing in a bowl game was a dream for the team and for the Wake Forest fans. Back in the '70s, there were very few bowl games, and they weren't branded by corporate sponsors. That year, North Carolina State University had won the Atlantic Coast Conference (ACC), but the University of North Carolina and Wake Forest University were the teams invited to bowl games, while the Atlantic Coast Conference Champion, North Carolina State, was not invited to play in a bowl game.

The night after our final practice, before the team was to depart for further preparation in Orlando, we held a team meeting. Because we would be in Orlando for a week before the game, a significant part of the meeting was going over the logistics for the week. As the instructions for the week were being outlined, team members who were not a part of the travelling team were informed that they would be going to Orlando on the bus with the Wake Forest University band rather than flying on the team plane.

This seemed strange and unfair. Everyone on the team had sacrificed and had given all they had throughout the season, only now not to have the experience of the entire team travelling together on the plane (which could accommodate everyone). That moment of dividing the team in this way has stuck with me all my life.

A member of the team who was a junior stood up and asked the question we were all thinking, "Why isn't the entire team flying to Orlando together?" From the corner of the room, I heard a scream coming from the head coach: "I'm mad!"

He ran to the front of the room, yelling at the questioner, "How in the hell do you think it's your place to question the plans that have been put into place?" The player stood his ground and stated, "Coach, even the non-travel squad has busted our tails all year to earn this bowl trip, and we deserve to travel together as a team, not be required to ride a bus with the band." The coach's face turned beet red and the veins in his neck bulged as he verbally went after the player.

He yelled, "You want to hear about sacrifice? I've sacrificed my family since back in the summer. They've suffered through this season while I've given all I have to this team. My family is riding on the plane with me so, no, there's not room for you!"

Not backing down, the player replied, "Coach, you've always said we were a family and now your decision clearly shows your priorities. At least, you can allow juniors and seniors who are not on the travel team to fly on the plane! We've put in years of time for this moment! Coach, I don't know about anyone else, but I think it's JUST WRONG!" The player sat down, and the room went dead silent. Finally, another coach stood and adjourned the meeting.

We went on to Orlando, had a blast, and got our butts kicked by LSU. But there was a bigger loss: The team that had come together and fought together throughout the year against all odds and predictions had been shaken by the true colors of our head coach, which were revealed during this meeting. While our commitment to each other as players remained, our commitment to our leader was gone. Our respect for him had evaporated as well.

 LESSONS LEARNED

1. Leaders are just people and they have stresses outside their professional roles. However, taking on a leadership role requires making the organization a high priority and being consistent.

2. Every member of the team, regardless of their position, is valuable as a person and deserves to be treated with respect (even the "walk-ons" in our lives!).

3. The true substance of a person is best seen when things go wrong, when pressure is at its height. These are situations when leaders go to what I've called their "root stock," when you get to see who they really are inside. Sooner or later, what sits in a leader's heart shows through, be it good or bad.

4. During times of stress and the worst of situations, organizations need challenges, but they also need re-enforcement and encouragement, with a large dose of "calm and collected."

5. Once the monster is out of the closet, it is nearly impossible to put it back. It's hard to forget the experience of seeing months of inspiration erased in a single 10-minute slice of time. Bad situations can be recoverable. However, they require humility and slowly rebuilding with many positive experiences, as well as taking ownership of poor decisions and expressing sincere apologies in words and actions.

THE MIRROR TEST

Questions for Self-Reflection

1. When have you had a team member in your workplace put you before themselves? If this has never happened to you, start a respect train! Be the first one in your organization to show how much you value others, regardless of their position.

2. If you've misspoken or acted in a way that you regret, did you take steps to correct your mistakes? If not, is there still time to do so?

3. Everybody has bad days, including you! On such days, what can you do to prevent your mood from infecting the morale of your team? Or, better yet, what can you do to pull yourself out of the negative space you've found yourself in?

CHAPTER 14

Opportunities in the Face of Uncertainty

In December 1996, I was responsible for the human resources organization for the North American consumer healthcare manufacturing division for my company. In addition, I was supporting the senior vice president of manufacturing, while continuing to work with the site director at our company's facility in South Carolina. I had a lot on my plate.

Since 1994, the company had designated the site in South Carolina for major expansion. We were to build out the campus and consolidate all of our consumer healthcare manufacturing within the United States in one location. From an organizational perspective, we had implemented some innovative and cutting-edge processes to organize and develop the organization to establish a true "manufacturing center of excellence" in South Carolina. The two years were a lot of work, but the work was exciting to build a cutting-edge organization to operate the most current technology of the day in the pharmaceutical industry.

We had organized the existing organizational structure of the South Carolina site into focused factories, based upon the value streams they supported, rather than the functional structure previously in place. The new design enabled functional areas and their leaders to be responsible for the end-to-end supply and align with their commercial colleagues. It also empowered the leaders to work entrepreneurially to manage the overall profit and loss (P&L) performance, develop funding for capital expenditures, create and agree on marketing strategies with their commercial partners, and develop the talent assigned to the focused factory/business.

Beyond the business alignment, the structure allowed for the development of leaders, technical experts, and operational employees around the established values and competencies defined to elevate the organization to the next level.

With this background of work already accomplished, including the selection of leaders for the focused factories through rigorous simulations and assessments at the center, I was scheduled for a meeting with the Aiken site director, Walt, and the senior vice president of manufacturing, Rob.

As we gathered in Walt's office, Rob kicked off the meeting with a simple and surprising statement, "The new president of global manufacturing, in partnership with Andersen Consulting [the original company later re-branded as Accenture], has made a strategic decision to scrap the plans underway to establish Aiken, South Carolina, as the U.S. center of excellence. Along with this decision, the company will begin the process of selling the Aiken site." You could have heard a pin drop.

Walt, who was toward the end of his career, had built this site and led it for 20 years. This news was particularly difficult for him to hear. He and I sat in stunned silence. Rob said, "I know this drastic change in direction is a hard message on many fronts, and you both have invested significantly in the former strategy to build out this campus.

Further, I know you have some questions, but to give you some time to reflect, I'll go through the next steps."

Walt and I were provided information on the next steps, and we were asked to sign a confidentiality agreement as this news and the sale process to follow needed to be managed carefully. The ongoing operations of the site could not be impacted by this decision. My mind was pinging with so many questions about the future, the site, the people I'd worked with for the past five years, and the path forward for my career and for my ongoing ability to support my family.

The interesting dynamic of being responsible for an organization of hundreds of people, and the personal impact on my family, consumed my thoughts. The question that rose to the top of my mind for Rob was, "What changed? All the work, plans, and messages we've been delivering over the past 18 months are now all reversed 180 degrees? I don't understand what changed."

Rob, who I admired considerably, said he had the politically appropriate response or the real response, and asked which one I wanted to hear. I told him I would need both. The political one will be necessary for future interactions, but personally, I was interested in the truth.

He agreed and replied, "Politically, the new president — in consultation with Andersen Consulting — has reevaluated the investment costs to build out Aiken, close the other sites, relocate and recruit people ... all in the context of the future growth projections of the business. The conclusion of that evaluation does not support the continuation of the strategy. Further, the commercial business has decided to focus on the oral care and the gastrointestinal business in the US."

I told him that I'd seen the numbers, run the future projections of the payback, and the numbers for continuing to operate in the current locations were favorable to continuing with the consolidation. Further, we had invested a million dollars in the build-out and the development of a new process for our leading gastrointestinal (GI) product. He acknowledged my business case and the development of the new and improved process but reiterated the new decision would result in the mothballing of this newly constructed facility.

I followed up by asking about the organizational impact on the Aiken site. We had made the decision to retain a workforce that was larger than the current level of business going through the site, because the future expansion would provide job security for that large of a workforce. This change would require steps to be taken for the financially viability of the site, and certainly to make it attractive to prospective buyers. Rob acknowledged this reality, and he said we would need to go through a workforce analysis and right-size the organization as a priority in the new year. My heart sank.

He then disclosed the non-political answer: the new president had bought totally into Andersen Consulting's guidance, which (in his opinion) was inappropriately influenced by the benefits Andersen would garner from shifting the strategy and embedding themselves into our organization. In short, the new plan was beneficial to the consultants. We continued to talk about the next steps and the process in which we would engage, along with the introduction of the project leader from the company and the Andersen people assigned to "work with us."

Later in the day, after Rob departed, the site director Walt and I met to discuss the news. He came right out and told me he was getting too old for this stuff, and he would be considering whether or not he would retire. I laughed and told him, "I'm not even close to 40 yet, so I've got to figure out what my future will hold."

He told me, "Your future will be determined by how you can learn from and use this upcoming experience to develop yourself. It's not what you had planned for, but with every change, opportunity exists." We then spent some time venting our negative reactions to the news, just to get it out of our systems, at least initially.

As I reflected over the Christmas Holiday the work I would face ahead in January, I had to get my mind and thoughts focused on the inevitability of the decision. I also had to get myself to a positive mindset regarding the news because the truth is that I have a pretty lousy poker face and I knew I couldn't operate like nothing was happening.

Through these reflections, the idea struck me: The business is being sold, but they didn't say who was buying it! Rob told us they would be seeking prospective buyers confidentially and would conduct a period of due diligence to determine the right buyer for the business.

Bingo! I could buy the business! This thought turned my mental focus away from doom and gloom, and from feeling like a victim of circumstances, to the possibility of taking proactive measures to affect the outcome.

From Leader to Owner

I spent several days mapping out a strategy regarding the steps I'd need to take to put together a solid business case to see if the purchase of the business would be financially feasible. I had to answer the question of whether or not the site could be successful as a standalone business, and what amount of upfront investment could be justified to acquire the site and start up a standalone business. I also knew I needed a team of individuals to participate in the work ahead, on our own time, because our plates were going to be full simply running the business and conducting the sale process. The next three months were going to be a significant amount of work, but I was convinced the opportunity was worth the investment of time and energy.

I solicited Rob to expand the team involved in the sale process to include an operational leader (Steve), quality and regulatory leader (Joe), and financial leader (Chuck) for the site. These roles were important to participate in the sale process and gaining approval for them to be involved would allow me to involve them in my initiative to put together a bid to purchase the site ourselves.

I talked to Walt about my plan, and he encouraged me to move forward, but cautioned me to be very careful about disclosing it before I was fully prepared to respond to the challenges I would receive from the company. I realized that playing a dual role of selling and attempting to buy the site would have to be balanced carefully. Walt also told me he was not interested in participating with the attempt to buy the business, but that he would support me.

I did ask him if he would be open to being named as part of the purchasing team, given that his tenure and experience would be a valuable addition in evaluating the credibility of our team. He agreed that I could use his name, but not to look for him to keep working if we were successful in purchasing the site. We agreed on the path forward. I received approval to bring in the other three members of the team into the sales process and I would be able to engage them in the secondary objective I was going to initiate.

As I called the meeting with the new team members and shared the news, I recognized they needed to go through the emotional adjustment to this radical change, just as I had done in December. I let this play out for several days before I asked them to join me for a meeting at the end of the day.

As we gathered, I had put together a few transparency slides (this was way before PowerPoint's introduction into the corporate world). I had run a five-year projection of the financials, given the upside and downside projections for the current portfolio of products being supplied by the site. Again, not yet having Excel, we relied on Lotus 1-2-3, which was the most effective tool before Microsoft became the dominant force in corporate software.

The kicker to the financial projections was the cost-savings potential we had in "leaning" the processes, process improvement to reduce variability, parametric release of products (release in real time), and eliminating corporate overhead costs that significantly impacted the P&L. Additionally, I shared with them the outline of employee ownership through an Employee Stock Ownership Plan (ESOP) of the business, designed to ensure everyone who came on board with us would have a minority stake in the business and an elevated commitment to our success. We spent three hours debating, agreeing, and refining the top line business case and its impact on the bottom line.

Further, the finance lead, Chuck, raised the reality that running a stand-alone business would be all about cash, what he termed "shoe box accounting." He and the other two members of the team enthusiastically agreed to join the team. I had prepared a confidentiality document, and an outline of our ownership agreements. We all had worked together for several years, but I told them that I believed that documenting our agreement from the beginning could be very important in the future. We agreed to meet on Saturday of that week and map out the full business case, and we all agreed that we would brainstorm on a critical aspect of moving forward, specifically how were we going to finance our bid to buy the business.

Over the next two months, we engaged in executing our day jobs and entertaining consultants, as well as the corporate team members that descended upon our site by the dozens. We all laughed that hotels and restaurants in our town had to be spinning with this sudden and lucrative influx of business and cash being spent seemingly out of nowhere. In parallel, and on our own time, we worked to refine our business plan further and further.

We identified real cost improvement opportunities and efficiency gains. We outlined multiple opportunities to employ the recently constructed and soon-to-be-mothballed pilot plant, which would provide an entire new revenue stream. We saw the opportunity to reduce the current supply costs the company was paying for products from the site to make our proposal very attractive to our commercial colleagues.

We spent a lot of time aligning on how we would lead and how we would build the culture of our organization, and we all agreed our future contract manufacturing business would be different from those we had worked with in the past. Specifically, we would break the current mold of selling contract manufacturing services to win the business, and then elevating the cost of supply with required activities that were not included in the original quotes. Let me explain ...

In short, during the '90s, the contract manufacturing sector of the pharmaceutical industry was notorious for getting its hooks into an innovator company and then layering on additional cost after cost. We decided we would offer a menu of services with prices and our own costs clearly identified. The premise was based on our belief that our future clients would be best served if we were successful, and we wanted to work in a transparent, open-book partnership with our clients.

Time was running close on the company's sale process; we were scheduled for a meeting to discuss the finalist list of prospective buyers of the site in three weeks. Fortunately, our business case and proposal were almost finalized, but we had a significant milestone to accomplish. We needed financing for our purchase. We were aware of our company's past sale of manufacturing sites to a management buyout (MBO), where the existing management teams were sold the business with ongoing supply agreements for just $1. While we hoped this route was a feasible one, the news that finalists were being identified sent a signal that we had to be prepared to offer a competitive bid.

I briefly had to focus my time away from my responsibilities for the company to seek potential investment routes for the funding of our bid. I solicited major banks in the Carolinas, and we set up a week for the team to meet with three different banks in Charlotte to make our pitch. We were pleased with the responses from the banks, and we were fortified by the economic conditions in the mid-90s. Cash was available, and our reception by the banks was well received during our days in Charlotte, as we went from bank to bank.

Ultimately, each bank was interested in some form of ongoing partnership in the business, and they were all insistent in the team holding a *minority* share and personally investing as well. Ugh! As we had dinner the final night over beers and burgers, the reality set in. Did we really want to be minority owners and sign up to be controlled by bankers who didn't have a clue about our business?

This development got me to thinking about the partnership prospect and the need for funds. I told the team, "It's clear that we can't do this alone because of the financing we want to put forward. The numbers that we had run and had aligned on showed that we can bear up to $7 million in financing and make the business work."

I said to them, "While we hoped we wouldn't have to take on that level of debt, we have to be prepared to offer it. So, if we are destined to take on a partner, why can't we select who that partner will be, and find a partner who would have a stake in the business beyond just funding?"

My three partners agreed, but a critical question loomed large: "Who would that be?"

I shared with them my observation that one of our largest costs in the business was for printed packaging components. Of all our vendors, our packaging supplier for cartons, labels, printed leaflets and brochures was the vendor with whom we spent the most. We had a great relationship with that vendor, and I had gotten to know the CEO very well over the past year. The last time he and I had met, he shared with me that they were exploring different ways to expand their business.

"What if I solicit a meeting with him next week during my vacation, by myself, so he won't feel like he's being put into an awkward situation with one of his major customers? Just think, if he's open to the idea, we have another opportunity to improve margins further by making the purchasing of our packaging needs internally through our business partner instead of externally." We all agreed that I would set up the one-on-one meeting.

The meeting with the CEO of our vendor was successful. We were able to reach agreement on all aspects of the business purchase plan. He even observed that our partnership would improve the cost basis of our business sufficiently to re-invest in marketing and sales. Further, he said his organization's commercial team could be leveraged to take on the task of growing the site's volume to exceed our projections for year two and three in our business plan.

We spent the day discussing and formalizing our plan. He asked if he could invite the leader of his business development group into our conversation. I agreed to this, if I had his word on confidentiality. He laughed and said he wanted to ask the same of me because he didn't want to jeopardize his relationship with the company. After all, he supplied packaging materials to all the company's sites in the US.

At the end of the 10-hour day, we struck a deal with a handshake and agreed that he would task his general counsel with drawing up the formal agreements of the partnership, ownership, and funding requirements. I felt a bit apprehensive in making the decision to proceed without the team's buy-in; however, we were running out of time and I was confident they would agree with the deal I'd struck.

When I got to the hotel, I called all three of the team members, not being able to hide my enthusiasm. Fortunately, they shared my excitement. We were on our way to buying our site and growing the business!

The week after my vacation, another milestone approached. We needed to set a meeting with the corporate project manager to present our business case and our offer for the site. We had to get this meeting set and established ahead of the naming of the finalists of prospective buyers. My request for the call with the project manager, who was based in the UK, was set under the non-specific heading of "questions regarding the Aiken site sale process."

During this time, email was very new, and we didn't have line speeds or mechanisms to share large files via electronic means. So, it was not unprecedented to make verbal presentations by phone with the commitment to follow up with documentation using intra-company mail. Finally, the time for the call arrived, and I was both nervous and excited about throwing our hat into the ring for the purchase of the site. I was confident that we had a solid business case that would be financially beneficial to the company and to ourselves. We had agreed to share some of our financials, but not our plans to drive additional margins beyond what we were offering up with our ability to reduce significantly our supply costs. In short, we weren't about to give away our winning strategy so it could be used without us.

I thanked the project manager for his time and jumped right into describing the work the team and I had completed to come to the table with an offer to purchase the site from the company. Now, there have been several moments in my life and career where my vision of how another person would react to a proposal or situation missed the mark, but the response I received from the project manager probably sits in the top five of, "not what I expected!"

He wasn't just unenthusiastic about our proposal. He was downright angry. He accused me and the team of undermining the whole project by not fully investing ourselves into the successful sale and later the transition to a new owner. He went on, in a threatening manner, to suggest that I had jeopardized my prospects of being retained by the prospective owners, and certainly had destroyed any prospect of being retained in another function by the company.

I was speechless for a moment, while the project manager began to pile on with his discontent. When he finished, I recognized that his primary motivation was to complete this project successfully. Beyond being successful with the project, I recognized that his reputation and career ambitions were the filters through which he was reacting to our proposal. I explained that we intended to compete as a potential buyer, with no expectation that the company would automatically endorse our proposal. What we were seeking was just a fair and thorough assessment of our proposal against those of other prospective buyers. We had no intention of sidetracking his success.

I told him my goal was to present our ambition to him ahead of the process of moving to the due diligence phase with the finalists, so we could be up-front and transparent. I also made it clear that our team had worked during weekends, holidays, and vacation time with an abundance of caution to ensure we didn't impact the business sale process or our regular duties.

Lastly, I shared with him the viability of partnering with a major existing vendor to fortify the seriousness of our position. He asked me who the vendor was, and I told him I was bound by confidentiality not to disclose the name of the vendor unless our proposal was formally accepted. With this, he ended the meeting and said he would have to consider what I had shared with him, as well as confer with other leaders in the company. He said he would get back to me in a couple of days, because the process to sell the business was close to finalizing the remaining parties of interest. I thanked him for his time and his consideration and said I looked forward to his call.

That evening, we gathered as a team for me to replay the conversation and its outcome. We were all so excited about the prospect of taking on the ownership of the business that I dreaded sharing the chilly reception with the team. In the end, we were all in this together, so I decided I couldn't spin the reaction any way other than to convey what was a seriously negative reception. After describing the conversation, I did offer the glimmer of hope that the company leadership might come back to us and accept our proposal.

But optimism aside, I was upfront in telling them I'd missed the view of our proposal from the project manager's perspective. In short, we'd thrown a monkey wrench into a plan that had been laid out and was well along in the process of being executed. The uncertainty for us just increased because we didn't know whether the company would remove us from our roles, from the process of hosting prospective buyers, or even immediately separate us from the company.

But perhaps they would see the logic that we saw in our taking ownership of the business. The next couple of days were nerve wracking, and we all kept our heads down and buried ourselves in running the business.

Four days later, I received the anticipated call from the project manager. He started by saying he was against the company's even considering or accepting our proposal. He told me that he honored his commitment and presented our initiative up the organization. He said that after much debate (and some anger and dissatisfaction with our pursuit), the company had agreed to accept our proposal and include us in the sale process.

I would need to get our business case and our official offer to him as soon as possible. He explained that over the next week, all the proposals of companies interested in the site would be reviewed and narrowed down to three finalists. He said he would keep me posted.

Whew! I felt a huge burden lift and a sense of relief. But the reality was that the political fallout of this move by our team was going to be tough to overcome, if it even could be.

Six days later, the follow-up meeting was set and I asked if the other three team members could be present for the conference call. They were allowed to join and we all gathered in my office. The project leader in the UK had assembled several company executives to be with him, as well as consultants from Andersen.

He kicked off the meeting saying, "The Aiken Team's proposal was presented late into the process, but it has been evaluated alongside all the other proposals. The decision based on review of all the proposals has been made not to continue with the Aiken Team's proposal as one of the finalists. We appreciate the work you've done, on your own, but we now must insist that the team apply all your efforts to host the finalists at your site. These visits will be pivotal to the finalists' preparing their last and final proposals."

He went on: "The company will not disclose the Aiken Team's involvement in proposing the site purchase because we don't want to negatively impact the sale, nor your potential prospects of being retained by the eventual buyer. Lastly, none of the four of you are permitted to disclose the work you've done to any of the finalists or to other individuals who haven't already participated or contributed to your proposal."

It was over and it was never to be spoken of again. It felt as if the wind had been knocked out of me again! I repeated the Serenity Prayer over and over in my mind. As the call closed, we went around the room and each person began to vent, as well as describe the project manager in colorful terms. In the end, we concluded that we weren't taken seriously in the process. We did own the fact that we should have engaged with the project manager earlier, and even should have involved him to a point that he could have taken credit for our work to his superiors.

Without elaborating or dwelling on the irony, the company ultimately decided not to sell the site. Further, the new president of the manufacturing division was summarily dismissed from the company, along with the Andersen consultants he had engaged in the execution of the changed strategy.

For me, I learned more about the financial levers that made our business successful, as well as the tools and methods we would have employed to later market the business and sell our manufacturing services. Ultimately, going through this process was a key enabler of my taking on the site director role when Walt retired. And, of course, I learned a great deal about myself.

Fast Forward a Decade

After the failed attempt to sell the manufacturing site I led in South Carolina, our site went through a difficult period of time. The commercial organization within the consumer healthcare sector of our corporation reduced the level of marketing support for the brands we manufactured and supplied them. Coming out of the sale process for the site, we were excited that our site would remain a part of the corporation, but our workforce was artificially larger than the business could support. In addition, the lack of marketing support for the brands resulted in significant declines in the amount of product we needed to manufacture.

My description of working with Anton really doesn't capture the challenges we worked through, but I'll encapsulate the essence of his leadership in the balance of this story. Within that particular corporation, and all I've worked in during my career, there was a pecking order of influence that was built by the relationships developed among individuals in powerful positions. Going back to before the year that the South Carolina site was going to be sold in the '90s, the leader of that initiative to sell my site continued to hold an interest in exiting the South Carolina site from the corporation.

Admittedly, I had burned a bridge with this person, but he continued to be retained at a senior level in the corporation, equivalent to Anton's. I always believed Anton provided political cover for me with this individual, which a leader does for talented team members who are fully committed and deliver results. For a number of years, Anton's supply chain and the overall consumer healthcare division were allowed to operate autonomously from the pharmaceutical division. John, the president of the consumer healthcare business, worked closely with Anton and he valued the manufacturing organization as a strategic asset for the commercial success of the business.

During John's tenure, our CEO recognized the unique differences between the consumer healthcare business and the pharmaceutical businesses. This understanding anchored John's and Anton's close relationship, despite Anton reporting directly to the president of manufacturing. It is pivotal to set the stage for how the corporation operated politically in order to understand fully Anton's leadership and his influence upon me, even though it is confusing to people not personally involved.

There was a change in the CEO of the corporation (and John's new boss), and soon to follow, John retired as the president of the consumer healthcare business. Through this period of change, a lot of the team that had grown the consumer healthcare business to exceed a billion dollars in sales began being disassembled. As the corporate leadership deck chairs were being rearranged and political alignments were placing new people in key roles, a very senior opportunity was created for Anton's peer — the precise person who had failed in exiting the South Carolina site from the corporation. He had regained a position of even greater power and influence.

These types of wholesale changes above are not uncommon in the corporate world, made worse by the unfortunate and unhealthy legacy of revenge and retribution held by some people in key leadership roles. Anton's peer leveraged his new position, as well as the changes in leadership and allegiances, to implement a strategy to prop up a struggling site by transferring successful product lines from my South Carolina site.

The call from Anton communicating the transfer of Aiken's manufacturing processes and equipment to the site that was struggling financially was difficult for us both. Again, to Anton's credit, he was professional and factually based as he presented the need for me to engage fully to facilitate the transfer that would lead to the demise of the organization and business I led.

I understood the dynamic situation Anton was in as a result of this shift in corporate politics. He outlined in detail the corporate script I was to follow, and then Anton asked if we could talk off the record.

Given my long relationship with him, I expressed my full confidence to Anton and said I was eager to hear what he had to say, knowing the message in his call simply was following through on directives from his superiors. He appreciated my confidence, and said he wanted to apologize to me for being out-maneuvered given the changes that had taken place within the corporation's leadership.

He committed that he would continue to support me and ensure any future site-related decisions would be made based on facts rather than on emotions or other motives. I'll always cherish Anton's confidence in me to share these insights, and I could feel his distress through the phone.

Ultimately, and again with a tinge of irony, a lot of time, effort and anguish went into the evaluation of transferring my site. When fully analyzed, the facts did not line up for the transfer to take place. Anton had exhausted his political capital through the process, and eventually he was replaced by his peer as the leader of our network.

Anton, many colleagues, and I recognized the corporation we had committed our careers to had changed into something we no longer recognized. But there is good news! While there are times when people succeed with motivations that would not hold up in the court of public scrutiny, leaders who never waiver from the right foundations ultimately will succeed.

While there are times when people succeed with motivations that would not hold up in the court of public scrutiny, leaders who never waiver from the right foundations ultimately will succeed.

Anton continued his positive leadership in a new corporation, and my career path continued wonderfully. During your career, it is likely you will look back to times when the team and the business owed their ultimate success to the leader. Thanks to Anton, our time together is one of those career highlights for me.

Have you encountered a situation that was initiated by a decision within your organization that you didn't understand? What steps can you take to gain a better understanding?

LESSONS LEARNED

1. To successfully operate a business, it is critical to invest time in defining expectations for leaders and employees at every level. View as an investment, not a cost, the importance of understanding the values of the organization, defining the competencies of leaders to lead by values, and the selection of the right individuals for the current and near-term business needs.

2. In the business world, personal relationships can override facts and data, especially when individuals involved are highly positioned.

3. Every experience can grow you and develop you, but it doesn't happen automatically. You mentally have to turn on this growth mindset, or you'll stunt your development and your career.

4. When you become so convinced about a path forward that requires other stakeholders to buy in, take time to evaluate the proposal from their point of view. You have to put your own thinking aside and evaluate the view of the other person — not how you *want* them to react, but how they likely *will* react.

5. Sometimes, you can derive learning and developmental benefits from the ultimate failure to achieve an objective, which will outweigh the disappointment over time.

View as an investment, not a cost, the importance of understanding the values of the organization, defining the competencies of leaders to lead by values, and the selection of the right individuals for the current and near-term business needs.

 THE MIRROR TEST

Questions for Self-Reflection

1. Have you ever put a lot of time and effort into a project or proposal, only to have it shot down immediately by your superiors? What did you learn from this experience? Did this eventually help you grow professionally and/or personally?

2. When developing a proposal, what steps should you take to ensure you have considered the expectations and motivations of the people to whom you will be presenting the proposal for approval or endorsement?

3. Have you encountered a situation that was initiated by a decision within your organization that you didn't understand? What steps can you take to gain a better understanding?

CHAPTER 15

Innovative Solutions with Clients

I'm guessing that, at some point in your personal life, you have experienced a shortage of a product you wanted to buy or, even worse, an out-of-stock situation. It's so frustrating to be ready to make a purchase and be told to "hurry up and wait" — maybe forever. Most of the time when we encounter these situations, the inability to procure something we want or need is simply an inconvenience. Often, we can find an alternative or substitute for the item we were looking to purchase, or we can find the exact item from another source. From a business perspective, however, not being in a position to meet the needs of customers or clients isn't good for the revenue stream. Worse than the financial impact, not having the product or service a customer wants to purchase from us can damage the business's reputation, which can be difficult or impossible to overcome. Customers complain on social media and tell their friends, or they simply flee to your competitor, never to come back.

There are, of course, industries (like healthcare delivery) that cannot allow their services to be cut off or their products to go out of stock because the impact on the customers goes above and beyond "inconvenience." But the truth of the matter is that, even when the product or service is a need versus a want, circumstances can still impact a business's ability to supply. Shortages happen in even the most unthinkable situations and the most vital industries.

I'm sure you've experienced a power outage at home or at work, during a storm or because of a major incident. Power outages are inconvenient for some, but downright perilous for others, like residents who use life-sustaining medical equipment that requires electrical power. Our utility companies in the United States maintain sophisticated monitoring systems and response teams to address power outages, and protocols are in place to restore power first to those whose needs are the greatest. I live in the southern United States near the Atlantic coast, so every year we experience the impact of significant storms and hurricanes, which can affect power supply even in the best-case scenario.

We all understand the uncontrollable events of nature that can impact the supply of a service or a product's availability. But think about the services provided by a hospital! It's hard to imagine a hospital that's not able to receive and treat patients, no matter how bad the weather is. The industry I worked in for the majority of my career, the pharmaceutical industry, is a lot like supplying power to a hospital. We could ill afford to allow our medicines to go out of stock, but sometimes it happened. Life-saving medicines can go out of stock for a variety of reasons, creating serious predicaments for the patients who rely on these drugs.

Preventing "Out-of-Stock" Situations

Not every out-of-stock situation is uncontrollable. In fact, in almost every company (perhaps including your own), it's easy to identify out-of-stock situations that could and should have been prevented by the leadership of the businesses. Often the reality of *controllable* situations that impact a business's ability to supply are the results of a series of events or decisions made over a period of time that finally come together. Each individual event or decision likely is reviewed and not considered to be a significant risk to supply; however, the cumulative effect of isolated low-risk decisions — when not recognized in time — can lead to catastrophic events. I want to share a story of a potentially catastrophic shortage of supply for a life-saving medicine that was avoided in a very innovative way.

The cumulative effect of isolated low-risk decisions — when not recognized in time — can lead to catastrophic events.

In 2011, I was hired to lead a large contract development and manufacturing site in Eastern North Carolina. The site's 600-acre campus had multiple facilities that manufactured drugs for other companies. For some of our clients, we partnered with them to provide the additional manufacturing capacity they needed to keep their products available for their patients. The supply chain of manufacturers for medicines that were absolutely necessary for patients' lives would normally have multiple manufacturing sites, located in different geographic locations. Each manufacturing site (also called supply nodes) would be capable of producing these drugs so that, in the case of a failure or interruption of supply at one site, another manufacturer could jump in to ensure the overall supply was not impacted. Our business also had many clients who used our business's ability to supply medicine as their *sole* manufacturer (meaning we weren't their back-up or overflow manufacturer, but the only company making their products). In these situations, we maintained multiple equipment trains and processes as back-ups to each other to ensure continuity of supply.

Shortly after taking on the lead role for this 1,300-employee organization, I immersed myself in learning the current state of the business. I needed to gain a sense of the current culture, the regulatory history (specifically related to audits scrutinizing our adherence to strict regulations),[1] the safety performance (e.g., accidents that resulted in an employee being injured on the job), the manufacturing processes we operated, the financial performance, the maintenance (mainly preventive maintenance performed), etc. Truly gaining an understanding of the overall performance history of the business was critical to gain insights into the work ahead of me as I led the organization and business through an improvement journey (which I was hired to do by the CEO of our company). Lastly, but just as important, I needed to gain an understanding of how the business was performing to meet our client's needs and expectations.

For me, the early days of taking on a leadership role has always been critical on many fronts — gaining insights into the historical performance, as well as seeking views and opinions from employees and clients. In every business I've joined, there has been a story (or stories) that emerges about past or current dysfunction, which becomes a challenge to overcome in order to gain the trust and confidence of the employees and clients.

While many themes of common beliefs or realities emerged from my initial investigation of the business, let's keep our focus on what it takes — from the vantage point of leadership — to prevent out-of-stock situations for our customers. One key theme that emerged during my initial sleuthing was the business's ongoing lack of investment in preventative maintenance of the equipment and infrastructure of the business. I heard story after story, and knew that this apathy about equipment and infrastructure was bound to eventually strike at the heart of the business's ability to ensure adequate

---

1 Being a supplier of regulated medicines throughout the world, our business was constantly being audited by the Food and Drug Administration in the US, the European Medicines Authority for European Countries, and other countries' regulatory agencies

supply of life-enhancing and life-saving medicines to our clients and their patients. This lack of investment, real or perceived, was developed over the years by employees and clients. I knew, from my experience, that the care of the tools, equipment, and facilities provided by the business would be a tangible opportunity to begin transforming the culture and the performance improvement I was hired to lead. Let's face it, if leadership is willing to "run equipment to failure" vs. proactively investing in maintaining it properly, those decisions are indicative of other decisions made by leadership. It's analogous to maintaining your car with regular oil changes — you know it has to be done, even if it's not convenient and not top of mind.

Let's face it, if leadership is willing to "run equipment to failure" vs. proactively investing in maintaining it properly, those decisions are indicative of other decisions made by leadership.

A Golden Moment

Beyond the input I received from employees and clients regarding the company's investment in maintaining the business, I had full access to the financial records of the business. From my review of the financial expenditures on maintaining our facility, I knew the business was spending a significant amount of money in both maintaining equipment and facilities and purchasing new equipment. The common belief among the employees and clients was a perception (so it was real in their minds), but the reality was the business's leadership was not spending money on the highest priorities. Additionally, the company was full of experts who could advise about high-priority infrastructure investments, but they had not been consulted. Likewise, management had not taken time to share and communicate where the business was spending money to maintain the equipment and facilities.

In one of my early Town Hall meetings (where I met with every person on site in a series of nine meetings, with 100+ people attending each meeting), I addressed the common belief that the business was not investing in the business. I shared with the organization how much and where the business was spending money and where we planned to invest further in the business... During the Q&A, I was challenged in nearly every meeting about a specific lack of investment in maintaining our infrastructure. This *specific* lack of investment in one particular area of the business was at the root of the belief held regarding the business's lack of *overall* investment. A truly golden moment emerged, offering an opportunity to begin reversing course regarding the business's culture and performance future.

This golden moment was described to me in detail by managers in the maintenance and engineering department during meetings I scheduled after the Town Halls to fully understand the situation. Specifically, the injectable, sterile-fill finish facility of our business was a major source of the supply of life-saving medicines. In the pharmaceutical manufacturing world, the manufacturing of injectable medicines in a sterile environment was the pinnacle of pharmaceutical manufacturing. This facility was 350,000 square feet, where we operated four different sterile-fill and finish-process trains. The drugs supplied from this facility included the most successful drug for the treatment of breast cancer, as well as many other life-saving medicines. The technical and scientific complexities of this facility were amazing!

Unfortunately, over the years, the managers of this business had put off, time and time again, the requirement to shut down the facility to perform the required maintenance on the infrastructure and equipment that fed electricity to the entire facility. Because the sterile facility has to constantly maintain environmental conditions to ensure sterility of the medicines produced (as the medicines are ultimately injected into patients who are very susceptible to infection), taking down the power source to perform the maintenance required would take a minimum of three weeks. Year after year, management had made the decision to delay this required work. When I took over leadership of the business, this necessary work had been delayed for five years running. While delaying a year (or even two) had moderate risk, the current state of the equipment caused by the delays had created a cumulative risk that was very high. The potential for a catastrophic failure of the equipment was extremely high and employees and clients knew about the risk. I knew this work had to be done! So we got started planning the shutdown immediately.

The facility was a critical source of medicines to many clients, namely the "who's who" list of pharmaceutical and biotech companies, such as Genentech, Merck, Amgen, Johnson & Johnson, and many others. The planning to shut down the facility, perform the maintenance, re-start the facility, and validate the return of the manufacturing environment to the sterile clean state was intricate and challenging. While the maintenance, engineering, operations, and quality teams were very capable to perform the task, our clients would also need to be involved in the work. Specifically, each client had to be informed and agree to the shutdown schedule, as our business would not be able to supply them with drugs during this period.

As the technical teams planned for the shutdown, I met with each one of our clients to communicate the plan for the shutdown of the facility. Each one of the clients knew and recognized that the work had been put off too long, and they were accepting of the time. Of course, given the criticality of the supply of these medicines, they also had to plan ahead to ensure their inventories were able to cover the loss of supply for the three-week period (or even longer, in case the three-weeks anticipated ended up taking longer). We also agreed to setting up meetings between our technical and quality teams and the client's teams, so they could sign off on the plans that were being established (and provide input from their knowledge and experience).

So, plans were forming, and our clients were all lining up to partner with us to perform this critical work. I made sure the organization was kept informed and knew I was committed to our organization performing this work. The follow-through on this commitment was a cornerstone to building trust and confidence in my leadership and my teams. Our clients were also appreciative of the commitment and our approach to ensure they were involved in the planning. Through the year ahead of the shutdown, the planning continued with regular updates on the progress of the procurement of materials, contractors, plans to secure very expensive inventories we held for clients, etc. The shutdown preparation was all on track, heading to the dates agreed upon in June of 2013.

An Unexpected Proposal

In March of 2013, with the planned shutdown just three months away, one of our client's other sources of supply for a life-saving medicine was cut off. My business was a backup supplier of this medicine, Doxil, for the client. Doxil was a cancer-fighting chemotherapy drug designed to help patients fight ovarian cancer. There had been a shutdown of the supply of an alternative to Doxil by regulators, so Doxil was the only available medicine for these patients who desperately needed the drug. At the same time the supply of the alternative to Doxil was stopped by the FDA, the primary manufacturer of Doxil for our client was also shut down by the FDA for violations of regulations established to ensure purity and sterility of the product.

Our client, the company that owned Doxil, was a division of Johnson & Johnson (J&J). The point of contact for my business and J&J requested a meeting with me and my commercial colleagues. The subject of the meeting was to delay the planned shutdown to perform the required maintenance of our sterile manufacturing facility. Throughout my short tenure of time leading this business, I'd heard of the past failures to commit and follow through on the required maintenance because "management prioritized revenue over doing the right thing!" I knew that this meeting and the request the client was bound to deliver was a scenario that had played out over the years, and past management of my business had scrapped plans to perform the maintenance. My team and I were committed to not going down this same path again, as we were close to executing the work and not doing so would risk our ability to supply all of our clients with medicine, as well as J&J.

We hosted the meeting with J&J on our site to hear their request. They were fully appreciative of our commitment to ensure we properly maintained our equipment and facility, and they understood the critical state that the years of neglect had created. Unfortunately, the client was also facing significant pressure to fill the void of supply created by their competitor's product being pulled from the market and the FDA's shutting down their primary supplier. The stakes were as high as they could be for their business and for ours, but more importantly, for those patients on a prescribed and rigorous treatment schedule for Doxil. Through the meeting, we all clearly understood the situation and, in the end, we closed the meeting without a solution we could all agree upon.

Personally, I struggled with the decision I had to make to reject J&J's request to delay our shutdown. Over and over in my thoughts, I couldn't get out of my head and my heart the potential impact to the grandmothers, mothers, wives, daughters, and friends who were fighting against their cancer and dependent upon the medicine we supplied. I continued to balance the needs of these brave women against the needs of the other patients' medicines we supplied — which could be at risk because of the previous decisions to delay the required maintenance. I prayed and prayed for guidance and the strength I needed to make the right decision for everyone impacted by this decision. Ultimately, I remained solidly committed to executing the planned maintenance, even though the potential impact of Doxil temporarily going out of stock continued to weigh heavily upon me and upon my team.

Two days after my meeting with our contact at J&J, I received a phone call from a very senior executive at J&J, named Mel. Mel and I had never met, so we went through our introductions on the phone and did our level best to get to know each other before digging into the matter at hand. Mel then asked if I could meet with him and his team in two days, and bring my technical and quality leaders to that meeting. He said his team would fly in to meet with us, if we were open to hosting them. I accepted his request for the meeting. I also shared with Mel my struggles with the situation and the impact on our patients (as I always believed J&J, and other clients' patients, were my own as well). He appreciated my sharing of my struggle, which he was wrestling with as well, and asked that we hold off discussing further until we were face to face.

With the meeting set, my team and I held many meetings to prepare. We had detailed plans of the work to be performed, descriptions of who was performing the work, contractors who had been hired, the schedule of equipment and parts necessary to be delivered on time, and coordination plans to ensure we were extremely efficient and precise in our planning and execution. My head of engineering and maintenance, Chris, was an extremely talented and bright individual, and he had led his team through every detail of this enormous challenge ahead of us. Chris was, and still is, one of the mentees and team members who I've been blessed to work with at several different businesses, and his team and plans were exquisitely technical and efficient to maximize the use of the precious time we had set aside for the work. In our preparation for the meeting, we aligned our agenda and documents that we would openly share with Mel and his team.

After engaging in initial pleasantries and introductions at the beginning of the meeting with Mel and his team, I shared the agenda we hoped to cover during the meeting. I admit, I was nervous, but confident. My senses were on high alert and I was filled with contradictory emotions and thoughts. I was attuned to all the messages being delivered in the meeting, words shared, tone, body language, and, just as importantly, seeing how Mel's team viewed him as a leader by how they watched him and reacted to him. I assessed Mel as a very capable leader who had earned significant respect from his team, and I knew the next few hours would pose a formidable task — maintaining my commitment to perform this necessary work no matter what we heard or saw in this meeting.

First on the agenda was Chris, who covered the major milestones of activities to take place during the shutdown. Each milestone was discussed and debated on its merits of criticality and the timing required to accomplish the work. Mel kept asking about the number of people and the skills of the people assigned for each task. Mel also asked insightful questions regarding the opportunity to perform multiple tasks in parallel to minimize the down time. Chris did a wonderful job in responding to inquiries regarding the planning and execution of the tasks, with the level of resources and skilled people we had available and who were assigned to do the work.

After going through the scheduled plan of tasks outlined to be performed, we broke for lunch. The break was a good time to step away from the intensity of the meeting, with everyone in the room knowing how high the stakes were for our companies and our patients. After lunch, Mel asked if he and his team could meet in a conference room by themselves. He said he wanted to talk through the planned schedule with his team. Of course, we accommodated Mel and his team for the time they needed.

When we came back together, I resumed the meeting by outlining the history of former leaders of this business jeopardizing ongoing supply of critical medicines by not properly caring for our equipment and facilities. I shared our struggle with this commitment, in the face of the potential for J&J's patients not having access to Doxil. I also shared openly with Mel and his team the reality of the multiple clients and their patients who could be at risk of reduced or unavailable supply of required medicines if we didn't address the maintenance needs.

I watched Mel and his team, and saw that their body language conveyed their understanding and agreement with everything I shared. Everyone in the meeting room was well aware of the high stakes we were dealing with, and we all had the knowledge of potential patient impact on our minds. As I finished sharing the position of our business, Mel thanked me for sharing these thoughts with him and his team. He then asked to address the team, which I certainly accepted.

Mel shared his team's collective appreciation for the detailed planning and work Chris and his team had completed. He said his team saw the work planned and how it was to be executed as being in line with how J&J ran their own shutdowns and maintenance work in their sterile facilities. Mel then recognized that our schedule was focused around a 12-hour schedule, based upon the number of skilled people and contractors we had available to perform the work. He said he trusted we were employing every person available to perform this work as safely and efficiently as possible.

Mel then made an unexpected proposal. He asked us to consider whether we could shorten the schedule of the work to be performed if we had more skilled and experienced people available to perform the work. As he paused after asking this provocative question, thoughts were bouncing around in my head at lightning speed. On one hand, was Mel challenging me and my team's full commitment of all the people we have available in our organization? For goodness sakes, the sterile facility was a large part of our business, but it was approximately 50% of the total business, so we had to ensure the balance of the business was also staffed. On the other hand, was Mel suggesting we hadn't properly planned and scheduled our shutdown in the most efficient way? Our business was large, but we certainly were not as large as J&J. Our business and J&J were worlds apart in terms of size and resources we could assign to this work. I restrained myself and my team from responding in a potentially combative way, and simply asked Mel, what he had in mind.

Mel smiled and his facial expression communicated he probably knew what I had been thinking during this pause in the conversation. He said, "Carson, J&J has nearly unlimited resources available to us. The supply of Doxil to our patients is the highest priority we have in J&J right now." He then proposed that J&J reassign skilled personnel from several of their sterile sites to come assist us, adding to our current number of team members assigned to perform work during the shutdown. He said that J&J would pay for all of the J&J employees' travel and living expenses ahead of the shutdown and afterwards to allow for employees from both of our companies to get to know each other and to make sure everyone was clear about their roles and expectations. Mel said, "Your team has done a great job in planning the shutdown, but your team has been constrained by the number of skilled people you have available. By adding the J&J team to yours, we can execute the shutdown over the full 24 hours in each day, with no wasted time."

WOW! What a unique proposal to introduce a client's technical staff into our organization. I knew my team had hundreds of thoughts and reactions to this suggestion. We were so close to starting the shutdown and this solution also brought in another set of challenges and stress. Before anyone on my team reacted to Mel's suggestion, I asked Mel if I could meet with my team alone in the room. Mel smiled with understanding, and he and his team gave us the room.

When the door shut, Chris was the first to speak, as he and his team would be impacted the most by the introduction of outsiders to the complex tasks ahead. We don't know these people, and what skills they have! Every pharmaceutical company works a little differently, and introducing different perspective right before we begin the execution of the shutdown brings a whole set of new risks, shared Chris. Our quality and regulatory leader shared his concerns regarding the level of training and orientation that we would need to provide the people from J&J to ensure they are properly trained and in compliance with our quality systems and policies. My leader of Environment, Health, and Safety shared his concerns about the training and oversight needed to ensure the people from J&J worked within our safety procedures and safety management systems. Around the room, the prevailing thought and reaction was against accepting this proposal and all the complexities it might bring. I let the conversation play out until everyone in the room felt that we had justified our position to reject the offer.

I had stayed silent and just listened and watched. When everyone had said what was on their minds, I asked them a question that was the only comeback I had for their very logical and appropriate approach. I asked my team to consider a different situation. What if, sitting in this room with us, were brave women and their family members who needed Doxil to fight off their cancer? "I know you all care deeply about the patients who ultimately benefit from our work, and I'm introducing this factor for you to reconsider

Mel's proposal," I said. The team sat silently, and I could read their thoughts that I'd just taken them from a focus on the work required to the real reason why we do the work we do. As the heads of my team began nodding, Chris spoke up and said, "I won't lie and say there aren't risks. We are increasing the preparation work load and oversight required during the shutdown. But if we are successful, the extra work is worth the potential success." I asked Chris if executing tasks over a 24-hour day throughout the shutdown happened, how much time could we save? He said he would have to review the current plan in detail, but his initial guess would be to reduce the 3 weeks to 2 weeks or maybe even down to 10-12 days. I asked the team, "Do we all agree to accept Mel's proposal and work with the J&J team to see if his idea could work?" They all agreed to move forward and explore the opportunity.

I asked Mel and his team to come back into the room. I thanked Mel for his innovative solution. I told him my team and I had discussed the proposal over the last hour, and we are unanimous in our agreement to explore his suggestion in more detail. I proposed that our technical teams spend the next two days mapping out a new schedule, sharing information about the skilled people J&J would bring to us, and present back to Mel and myself their new plan after they'd had time to work together on the new plan. Mel and his team nodded in agreement, and they all shared their commitments to work closely with my team to ensure our success.

Creative Collaboration

Over the next two days, the combined teams worked closely together to develop an expedited plan that would reduce the shutdown to 14 days at worst, and 10 days at best (so Chris's initial assessment was right on the mark). They presented the plan to Mel and me, and we all committed to each other to make this happen.

In the weeks leading up to the shutdown, planning continued, along with orientation and training required by the J&J team members who would join our team. We also used this time to communicate this plan to our other clients, with an emphasis on ensuring we had put into place controls to prevent the J&J team from seeing any of their intellectual property my business held. We also accepted other clients who requested to have oversight of the work being performed by their technical experts, which we worked out with them and our team.

The shutdown was a success! Chris and his team coordinated and led the shutdown flawlessly. There were huddle meetings every day at 7:00 a.m. and again at 7:00 p.m. to go over the tasks completed by the shift leaving to go home and the tasks ahead of the shift that was coming to work. There were points shared by all team members and recognition of each other's work during these huddle meetings. The spirit of all the people in the room was electric and positive as people shared and complimented each other about how their fellow team members helped each other to work safely. This huge task was completed in 12 days by this combined crew of skilled people from two collaborating companies who had one shared goal. Beyond the outstanding accomplishment, the combined teams had developed close bonds and our clients who observed and participated saw first-hand how much my team cared about them and their needs.

We held a barbecue at the close of the shutdown to celebrate and recognize the monumental task of the shutdown. The celebration was also a farewell to our new friends, who departed with significant respect and pride in each other and what we'd accomplished together. The supply of Doxil remained in stock, and no patient who was already in treatment went without receiving their needed dose. A few weeks later, Mel and his team returned to our site to hold a celebration of this accomplishment with the entire organization (including operators who did not work during the shutdown, but were responsible for manufacturing Doxil on a daily basis). Mel shared the positive impact everyone in my business was making by telling stories about specific patients who were benefiting from our team's work.

Mel and I continued to build upon our relationship and we remain good friends today. In fact, I've had other opportunities to work with Mel and his team with other businesses I've led after this wonderful accomplishment.

 LESSONS LEARNED

1. A mindset shift can change everything. For a team to accomplish a goal sometimes requires a different perspective, which can allow individuals and the group to overcome objections and fears, and to change their thinking. Strong leaders know when to remove themselves from the details of tasks to recognize the "big picture." Knowing how and when to do this is a critical instinct and skill to develop.

2. Innovation is a product of need to be fulfilled when there is no apparent solution.

3. Change, unplanned events, and external influences cannot always be controlled, but you have full control over how you respond.

4. The value of partnerships is enormous, specifically when you have a common goal and different views on how to accomplish the goal.

THE MIRROR TEST

Questions for Self-Reflection

1. Have you experienced a time when you were "locked into the forward path" and missed an opportunity presented by others?

2. Can you think of a time when a description of a situation sounded accurate, but the reality might have been different from the conventional wisdom (i.e., the common understanding or belief) of the organization?

CHAPTER 16

Build Two Resumes

What? Build two resumes? Creating one resume and keeping it current is tough enough, even in the day of LinkedIn!

Hold on, I'm not suggesting you use a different resume depending upon the targeted company you may want to join (although a bit of focus toward a sought role is acceptable). All professionals have been required to put together a resume that documents our work and education history. The better resumes I've reviewed go beyond the description of jobs held, and focuses on the accomplishments or value delivered in each role a person has performed — the "so what" about the "what I know" or "what I've done." For the professional resume, I always have screened out resumes that don't immediately communicate to me what value I could envision someone bringing to my organization. I've always looked for — in resumes and in interviews — the answer to this question: "If you were a business, a product, or a brand, what would your marketing billboard communicate?" The professional resume should be pointed and focused on what you want to sell about yourself (and it's ok to be a bit of a narcissist, as we all know most, if not every accomplishment, is a product of a team's efforts).

I always have screened out resumes that don't immediately communicate to me what value I could envision someone bringing to my organization.

Oops, I apologize for getting into "Resume Writing by Carson!" This story is about the other resume I've hinted about, and the power of using this tool for yourself (and potentially others). In a moment, I'll get into the genesis of this tool, which was a result of a stressful time (but a good time) in my career. First and foremost, the second resume — "Your Personal Resume" — is about your avocations, not your vocations! Throughout my life and career, I have had this scripture come to mind from the Bible's Book of Luke: "To whom much is given, much will be required." Giving back is not something we have to do, but giving is something I feel called to do. I was fortunate to volunteer as a football coach for a local middle school, which was a great opportunity to coach young people in the skills of football (and some life skills as well!). One of my favorite roles was leading the Community Free Medical Clinic. Along with the Clinic's Board of Directors, we were able to expand the reach of quality medical care to people in our community who could not afford care. Lastly, if you'll indulge me, I saw a need and desire for the people who worked at my manufacturing site to make a difference in our community. We established a "day of caring" where each person was expected to volunteer (and be paid for eight hours) in their community. We took on major projects each year to provide opportunities for employees who hadn't identified anywhere to volunteer. One year, our county had finished the construction of a new elementary school building. The county had not planned on a way to move furniture, equipment, etc. from the old school building to the new one. The people who worked at my site literally moved a school!

Yes, I've fully invested in my career and delivering value to my organizations and the individuals who I've been blessed to lead. The delivery of value is wholly satisfying, but the opportunity to help our society and others by employing skills and talents is the opportunity we all have to define ourselves! Engaging my entire organization in volunteerism was also powerful in establishing the importance in our community and the people who worked at my site. Throughout my life, I've looked for and acted upon opportunities to volunteer and support others.

So what value is there in building a second resume? I'll provide my answer before I get into the story of why I developed the tool for myself. The exercise of thinking through who you are, what your life priorities are, and physically writing them down is a powerful one. It's a lot like looking at yourself in the mirror and asking yourself, "Did I give everything I had to give today or not?" This tool is for you to keep, and it will evolve over time as you develop and mature through the phases of life. Now, onto the story!

I was very content in my role as site director of the pharmaceutical manufacturing site. Every day was exciting and the days were full of opportunity to learn and grow, while contributing to our organization and business in a positive manner. At this point in time, organizational changes were taking place in the corporation that owned the site I led. As changes took place in the leadership of the corporation, I was disappointed to see the president of global manufacturing for the organization retire his post. I had great respect for him, and we had developed a good relationship. In that year's Global Leadership meeting for the corporation, our new president was introduced and he presented to the organization his vision for how the manufacturing organization would support the overall business in the future. The new president was a dynamic and inspiring speaker. His vision of what our organization could accomplish was a view that I saw as logical, stretching, and achievable. I recognize I trust quickly (or until trust has been broken), and I was quickly all in! As the weeks progressed, I had the opportunity to meet with the new president, David. He was very engaging and curious, asking thought-provoking questions and taking what appeared to be a genuine interest in my perspectives. We talked about his vision for the organization, and he sought my views and vision for my part of the business, as well as feedback on his vision for the global organization.

Over time, I was honored to have developed a close relationship with David. As we developed and invested in our relationship, I cherished our interactions and insights. Relationships are critical to careers, and building who we are as individuals, and I will always hold in high regard David's taking the time to invest in our relationship. He led an organization of more than 20,000 people and I respect that his time was precious and valuable. Throughout our conversations, David would ask me to connect with different colleagues who he had met during his tours of sites from around the world. My unique background in taking on the site leader role for a pharmaceutical manufacturing organization from the HR profession aligned with others David had met, who had different backgrounds and similar career ambitions. I was able to develop a mentoring relationship with several individuals from around the world, and each one grew mutually beneficial relationships. Each of the individuals have been successful in growing their careers. For example, Ervin transitioned from human resources into a site director role. Following his success as a site director, he moved into the quality profession and he's been elevated to the executive level in his company.

Another topic became a regular point of discussion when David and I would speak. He knew I had turned down roles that would relocate my family from the only hometown my sons had ever known. Sandy and I had committed back in the '90s to not seek opportunities that would require relocation. David told me he took it as a mission to grow and develop my career, and the opportunities I could take advantage of would necessitate relocation. I continued to share with David that I would be very open to these opportunities after my youngest son graduated high school and went away to college. This response worked for a couple of years.

My eldest graduated high school and went away to college and my youngest was a couple of years away from graduating when I received a meeting request from David's assistant. The formality of it struck me as different, and the subject was "Carson Sublett's Opportunities and Relocation." David had finally come to the point where it was time for us to finalize our discussion regarding my career, and I suspected there was a specific need David had within the organization. I was still a couple of years away from committing to opportunities that would require relocation. That afternoon and evening, the dilemma weighed on my thoughts. The question I had to answer: "How can I properly communicate to David my life priorities right now?" I'll always recall waking up around 4:30 a.m. the next morning with the idea of putting together my personal resume to proactively share with David ahead of our conversation. This idea, while simple, kicked off a significant time of self-reflection.

At first, I asked myself to answer the introductory question I'd answered many times in meetings and business gatherings. Who is Carson Sublett? The typical response a majority of people provide when asked to introduce themselves is their job title, who they work for, how long they've worked in the role, and possibly other roles they've held, or even the school they attended. This question took me down a path of consideration: "Am I the position, or the person who happens to be employed in the position?" I'm not testifying as to what the right or wrong answer is for everyone; however, for me, the answer is clear. I am not my professional title. I believed myself to be a professional; however, I held priorities in life ahead of my paid role. I began to list my life priorities, roles, identities: a Christian, a husband, a father, a son, a brother, a volunteer coach, a leader of a free medical clinic in our town, a friend, and on and on. For each one, which became my avocational roles, just as a career resume lists vocational roles, I developed a list of accomplishments and goals. As I put the list together, the proverbial chronological order didn't make sense; so I needed a different format and structure. Of course, my personal resume's roles should be listed in the order of priority in which I held them. I spent the appropriate amount of time to ensure the document communicated who Carson Sublett is and, most importantly, the priorities of my life right now. Of course, my professional role was also included, as I always held my professional role as a part of who I am as a person. The following day, I emailed the document to David. In the cover of the email, I told David that the attachment helps to outline who Carson Sublett is today and my life priorities. I respectfully asked that he read the document, which I would cover during our upcoming conversation.

"Am I the position, or the person who happens to be employed in the position?"

The following week, the time for our conversation finally came. I called David's office and his assistant put David on the line. He initiated the conversation with a laugh! *("Oh no, have I blown it,"* was my thought.) David then told me he had never seen such a document. He went on to tell me that he'd thought many times about his life's priorities, but he'd never gone through the exercise of putting them down in writing. He said he was impressed, but he was also prepared to make a pitch to me regarding a relocation opportunity. He admitted, after reading my personal resume, he might be wasting his time, but he wanted to pitch his idea anyway.

His pitch was well crafted and very enticing from a professional level. He even personalized the pitch from his own experience and the value his children had derived from the opportunities to live in different countries around the world. We talked at length about our lives and our life priorities. In the end, David recognized I remained committed to deferring relocation opportunities until my youngest son went away to college. I'll always hold David dearly in my thoughts and value my connection with him. His pushing me to analyze myself and my priorities resulted in a valuable tool that I've continued to build and develop over my life. David and I remained close, but over time our interactions became fewer and fewer. Ultimately, after my youngest went away to college, I did seek and found a great career opportunity. Sandy and I did relocate, but not too far away from our sons. Years later, David and I connected again on a philanthropic initiative David was engaged in, and it was good to be back in touch with someone who ultimately came to know me so well.

In the end, it's about knowing *yourself* well. And sometimes that self-awareness takes a little homework, like the exercise of writing a personal resume or developing a similar tool. The personal resume became a cornerstone in my future efforts to mentor and develop others for years afterwards. I maintained and updated my personal resume as life events changed and priorities shifted. For example, as my sons graduated from college, they remained a top priority for me, but the focus shifted toward friendship and mentorship with them. The exercise and thought required to develop and maintain a personal resume is powerful for people who make the time to do it, regardless of your role or profession. Even if one never shares their personal resume with anyone else, the tool will be a valuable one to shape and grow your life!

LESSONS LEARNED

1. Self-analysis of life priorities grounds us as individuals and helps us each truly see who we are as a person, beyond a role that we get paid to perform.

2. Life priorities evolve because life is not static. Keep updating, keep adding value, and keep challenging yourself to use your talents and capabilities to better your community, schools, and others in your life!

3. Other people in your life will benefit from your talents and skills, so share!

4. Prioritizing your life (vocations and avocations) ensures you invest your time to accomplish these priorities and fully engage yourself as a person.

THE MIRROR TEST

Questions for Self-Reflection

1. What talent or gift do you possess that you can share and help someone else in their life's journey?

2. Think about who has influenced you. What key attributes have you adopted from them?

3. Have you influenced others, and what key attributes have they adopted from you?

RESULTS OF A LIFE OF EXPERIENCES

Leadership Foundations

When we think of "foundations," we think of where we start — what's below the surface, what matters most, what comes first, what makes us strong and capable, what remains true even when lives and careers are changeable and unpredictable.

So why would I conclude this book with the foundations that have formed the bedrock for my career in leading organizations? Because I know many of you who are reading this book are just beginning your careers. Maybe you've already been identified as an "emerging leader" or a "high-potential employee" or a "management trainee." Or maybe you are still below the radar, observing and learning and preparing to take your professions or industries by storm. And to do so, you'll need a solid foundation. Perhaps I can loan you some of mine.

For as long as I can remember, the five foundational beliefs and actions outlined below and alluded to in the stories that have preceded this closing section of my book have guided my work and life, my decision making, my communications, and the experiences I endeavor to create in all my interactions.

In every organization where I've been hired as a "boss" — and where I hoped to *earn* the label of "leader" — I've presented these leadership foundations to my teams.

Why? First, people need to know what makes you tick. If you've been hired as their boss, they're going to need to know something about you if they are going to successfully support you. Second, leaders need their organizations to provide them with feedback. Third, when you set the expectation bar for yourself through clear and solid foundations, it can indirectly set the bar for the entire organization.

FOUNDATIONAL BELIEFS

Here are my five foundational beliefs that are the basis for my leadership:

Actions + Decision = Words

(The Trust Equation)

People are uniquely developed to have a sense of whether or not someone is genuine. I've fondly called this capability the BS radar. We develop it through our life experience, and learn to detect through reading body language, tone, and the words people use. Sure, some individuals are more tuned into their BS radar than others, but those who are highly engaged can identify clearly the genuine nature of an individual. Consistency is critical for a leader.

Honesty is Non-Negotiable

Whether the message is an easy one or a tough one, people want the truth. People deserve to hear the truth, which empowers them to respond to the message in their own way. One of the worst things to hear from a team is "I wish I had known what we were facing and had the opportunity to do something different to change the outcome we are *now* facing."

Feedback is THE Essential Tool
(To Receive and to Give)

Every person has blind spots. Think about it. We can't see ourselves, outside of a mirror or a selfie. We can't hear ourselves, nor can we surmise what others are thinking unless we ask!

Conversely, we *can* see and hear others. Feedback is a gift for you and others to act upon, reflect upon, or ignore. We should never withhold or resent the gift of feedback! In fact, sincere feedback should be a trigger for self-reflection. One mechanism, although it feels odd in the beginning, is to lock yourself in a room with a mirror, stare into the eyes looking back at you, and ask yourself two simple questions:

- "What did I do today that I am proud of?" and
- "What did I do today that I could have done differently or better?"

Looking into those eyes is a sobering experience, as there is no bluffing the person in the mirror! How you answer and, more importantly, what you do as a result of the answers will mark you as a person and a potential leader.

We should never withhold or resent the gift of feedback!

Everyone Wants to Be Successful

Some of you already are thinking, "Well, I know someone and they really seem content at the bottom of the food chain at work." Or

"Not everyone is ambitious." Or "There are plenty of people who don't need 'success' to be happy."

Don't be fooled by someone who attempts to preserve their own self-esteem by self-deprecation! Everyone I've known in my life wants to be successful. The definition of success is as varied and diverse as we are as individuals. But we all want to succeed.

The corollary to this belief is that people want to be part of successful groups — organizations, teams, families, etc. The best organizations I've worked with had cultures in which we always looked to the team for solutions instead of focusing on the problems. As a leader, if you create an environment where ideas are welcomed and tried, where successes are shared, and where unsuccessful attempts are learned from, your organization is going to win.

As a leader, if you create an environment where ideas are welcomed and tried, where successes are shared, and where unsuccessful attempts are learned from, your organization is going to win.

Every organization has the ideas necessary for it to be successful.

The Ideas Are Here

In every company I've worked with, we've encountered challenges. The focus of business today is dominated by continuous improvement. I've yet to face a challenge that was not successfully overcome through the experience and ingenuity of the collective capability of those who make up the organization.

As a leadership foundation, the right environment has to be in place for people to bring forward their ideas and plans. The acceptance and enhancement of ideas through recognition is critical. While not all ideas succeed or will be put into use, the exploration and evaluation of them sends a message to the organization. People are important, and their input is not only desired but required!

As you have now seen my leadership foundations and read the high-level background about why I hold onto them, think about your own! Who are you as a leader? What beliefs ground you? Knowing your foundational beliefs is very important. Once you've established your foundations, they will be tested by events and circumstances. They can adapt and evolve, but they should remain in place and not be compromised by future situations you face.

Key Responsibility of Leaders

There is no perfect formula for leadership nor is there such a thing as a perfect leader. But, as I reflect upon the opportunities I've been afforded in my career, I think I've done a good job of rising to the occasion when times got tough, when teams and organizations needed me, or when a dose of creativity, fresh perspective, or some extra humanity might make a real difference in solving problems or paving a new path forward. Being a leader is a big job that can be approached with a relatively simple mindset as you face highly complex and dynamic situations. I've focused on three areas in my career to earn the label of "leader."

Leadership – Three Areas of Focus

1. **Right Team** – Teams are either dynamic and growing, or they're dying. The right person in a role today may not be suited for that role in the future, including the leader. Developing and sometimes changing team members is an ongoing area of focus. It's important to note that making changes doesn't imply that the people impacted by the changes are "bad" people. They just might not be the right person for the role at that time in the organization's life.

2. **Environment for Success** – It's vital to ensure the team has the tools, training and, yes, the culture necessary to achieve the success goals of the organization and for themselves as individuals.

3. **Clarity of Success** – Every team member needs to go beyond knowing or memorizing the vision, mission, and success goals of the business. They need to be able to articulate the strategy and, most importantly, know how they and their team contribute to the achievement of success. In short, build teams with the knowledge to take on full ownership and accountability. When people know where they fit and how their work impacts the whole, everyone benefits and everyone succeeds.

I struggled for many years to describe my responsibilities. My not being a scientist, an engineer, a mechanic, or a member of some other profession whose contributions are more readily understood by others has required that I create my own vocabulary, tools, frameworks, foundations, and areas of focus to ensure that I'm performing well. The responsibilities of a leader — these key areas of focus (right team, environment for success, and clarity of success) — differ from functional accountabilities, such as profit and loss, safety, or quality performance. But they are no less important, no less measurable, and no less teachable (which is why I have written this book for you).

If you are already a leader or are aspiring to become one, I'm convinced that concentrating on these key areas continuously should be your job description. When asked what you do as a leader, you perhaps couldn't do better with an answer than, "I take responsibility for assembling and maintaining the right team, creating an environment for success, and ensuring every member of the team has clarity about how we define and achieve success together."

Don't be afraid to rethink how you approach any or all three of these key responsibilities of a leader. They are never set in stone. Their dynamic nature is always evolving and developing. Any organization or team you may lead is as complex and dynamic as the individuals inside it. How people interact with each other, what they are facing outside of work, how they feel on any particular day, and other factors impacting their lives all get incorporated into the culture of your team, organization, and business. Having clarity of what you focus upon, on top of your foundational beliefs, will enable you to lead.

If you're reading this and thinking, "I already have these areas of focus down to a science. I'm good. In fact, I'm a great leader," I applaud you. But I'd offer a word of caution: Your ability to positively lead an organization is earned daily, so the constructive impact you have made in the past is perishable. That reality requires a constant stewardship of these areas of focus. Every day, and in every way. Conversely, no one has ever expected perfection of others (unless you're a referee of a sporting event or a judge in a contest), but we do expect you to continually strive for and work toward perfection!

A closing thought from me to you ...

May the gift of logic, the practice of self-reflection, and the willingness to apply the lessons of your experiences allow you to make good and decent decisions that, in time, earn you the opportunity and privilege to be called a leader.

LESSONS LEARNED

A quick-reference collection of Lessons Learned from Chapters 1 through 16.

Bosses are Hired ... Leadership is Earned

1. People understand the boss/subordinate relationship, but what they seek is a leader who understands three simple truths:
   - Everyone, regardless of their job title or duties, wants to be successful.
   - When subordinates are successful, the business is successful — and so is the leader.
   - BOSSES ARE HIRED ... LEADERSHIP IS EARNED!

2. Successful leaders provide specific and direct feedback in a respectful manner. They praise in public and critique in private. But just as importantly, leaders seek specific and direct feedback from their team.

3. If you are appointed or already hold a supervisory role, people listen to what you say. But more importantly, they watch what you do. A simple formula for success is:
   - My Decisions + My Actions = Trust

4. People want to hear the truth from their boss. Not all messages are what people want to hear, but they need to hear them all. Honesty is non-negotiable!

It's What People Don't See

1. We always have a choice to blame someone else for unfair circumstances. But in doing so, we relinquish our lives to the control of others.

2. The one person you cannot lie to is looking back at you in the mirror.

3. Listening to feedback from others is a gift to cherish and use. What you do with the feedback is a choice you own.

4. Hard work and personal investment can overcome the limitations of your talent, enabling you to be the all-star of your life!

Good Bosses, Great Leaders

1. Great bosses give you the freedom to make mistakes, but they will not allow you to fail.

2. You have to own your own career and development. Passively waiting for something to happen or for a "big break" to fall in your lap will stagnate you.

3. Know your strengths but be humble enough to admit your weaknesses. Use this knowledge to build a team that covers all the bases. Develop your weak spots, while building on your strengths.

4. To build a team, you have to invest in being a team. Yes, you need common objectives and goals, but you also need experiences shared together that are outside the confines of the

work environment. In short, you need to focus on building relationships.

5. Leaders who focus on the development and growth of their subordinates also grow and develop from their team. Good leaders are constantly developing and growing their organization's succession plan.

6. Leaders can create an environment of healthy competition within the team, while maintaining solidarity toward the goals of the entire team and the business.

7. Leaders can coach and develop you by how they conduct their lives, both in the workplace and personally.

Leadership Can Be Lonely

1. Organizations respond to the leader. If a leader panics, the organization panics. If a leader is calm, the organization is calm. As a leader, you sometimes have to be able to separate yourself from your feelings.

2. When facing extreme adversity, simple instructions allow people to focus and contribute.

3. Any organization is a sum of individuals who become connected as a single being that will pull together or apart on the basis of how they are led.

4. The resilience of a team will be tested and these times of testing will form the character of the organization and its leaders. This character ultimately is reflected in the performance of the business.

Organizations Deserve the Truth

1. People in an organization need to be informed about how the business is performing. In the case of this particular manufacturing plant, providing truthful, tough messages could have allowed the people who relied on this plant for their livelihoods to have made the necessary changes. While it only might have delayed the final outcome, at least they would have had a fighting chance.

2. Never underestimate the impact of ego, or the fear of change in some individuals. The plant manager, who had been very successful for decades, took the proposal for change as a personal affront, ignoring what the business needed. In difficult situations, sometimes good people with decision-making authority just make bad decisions.

3. Recognize what you can change or influence, and focus your attention on those areas. For aspects of work or life that you can't change, simply accept them and become effective in how you deal with them.

4. In every life or career, there will come a time when you have to make personal decisions for your own welfare and that of your family. In this instance, I saw the disaster that was coming, and I reached out to the broader organization for opportunities in other parts of the business. One of the saddest duties that I had was volunteering to return to this site to perform exit interviews with as many of the employees as possible following the corporation's decision to shut down this old factory. It felt like an "I'm sorry" along with a "goodbye."

Leaders Have Issues Too

1. Some individuals can achieve significant positions of influence despite integrity flaws.

2. Assessment of leaders and talent is an inexact science, and character flaws can manifest themselves at unexpected times. How you react as a leader or a person when these character flaws surface is all you can control, so worrying about the actions of others who you don't influence is a drain of energy and simply unhealthy.

3. Unfortunately, politics is played at every level in every organization. Your radar has to be tuned to the nuances of words and actions, while not allowing yourself to read a conspiracy into every situation, but remaining conscious of the multiple layers of maneuvering that can take place. It's a balance that requires experience as well as the recognition that your view of a workplace situation is likely to sometimes be inaccurate. Regardless of how awkward the situation, you have to verify or challenge your thinking. It is better to address than to assume — at least some of the time!

Believe in What You Do

1. To be a leader, you have to be able to inspire. To be genuinely inspirational, you have to believe in your business, organization, or team. In short, if you're not inspired by what you do, you won't be able to inspire and lead others.

2. It is vital to connect individuals to the whole (the whole team, the whole organization, the whole industry ecosystem, the whole mission). One attribute of a successful organization or team is the ability to see how the collective results of everyone's efforts

deliver what could never be delivered by one individual, or even a machine. As we are facing the growth of artificial intelligence in our world, the differentiation of the combined focus and investment of people working toward a commonly held belief will become more and more important.

3. Leaders must create an experience that people buy into and believe. How do you want your colleagues or team members to describe what they and their organization do when they are having dinner with family or friends? A leader has to provide information and experiences for individuals to grab onto and own. Everyone seeks a sense of purpose. The opportunity to contribute to a mission that is genuine and believable is a critical step to achieving the goals of any organization.

4. The "what have you done for me lately?" attitude in business has always been in place, but the timeline to answer this question continues to compress. Every day (realistically every hour) can make a difference, so leaders must inspire their organizations to act daily in accordance with this reality!

A Culture Exists: Is It the Right One?

1. To influence a change, a leader must invest time to understand the current state of the business and culture before communicating future changes. You will have to be a listener and an observer, and seek validation of views formed before articulating your assessment.

2. A leader who needs to initiate a change must earn the right to do so and to be listened to by the organization. Again, you've been hired as a boss, and the people will award you with the label of a leader (or not) based on your behaviors, actions, and decisions.

3. Seek and find leaders and unidentified influencers of the organization and validate their standing amongst the people of the organization through diligence of point #1 above.

4. At the right time, communicate what you've found in an inquisitive, non-accusatory manner. Seek to understand, not to embarrass or call out.

5. Be prepared to make quicker changes with more senior-level employees, specifically those who don't recognize the validity of issues most of the organization sees. What I'm talking about are issues that others talk and laugh about (openly or in small groups) in a sad and sarcastic manner — those are the issues that many senior-level employees are blind to, but the "I told you so" people in your organization use as tools.

6. Successful cultural transformations are embedded when the people pull the changes into their teams rather than having those changes forced upon them or pushed by bosses. Recognition of the impact of culture on the success of individuals, teams, and the business must occur within key influencers of the organization.

People Are the Solution, Not the Problem

1. Some leaders look at their people as a problem, while successful leaders view people as the solution!

2. The ideas on how to improve a business are known by the individuals who perform the work on a day-in and day-out basis. To unlock those ideas, people need to be valued as relevant, and be confident their ideas will be received and evaluated.

3. If you want to communicate to someone that they are important, go to them in their work area, listen to them with

genuine interest, and then follow up. The first two actions reinforce and validate the third, which communicates "You are
important to me."

4. There are some individuals in supervisory roles or even functional roles of expertise (e.g., engineers or accountants) who
   don't yet know how to engage and interact with people effectively. Coaching, sharing, and setting a positive example for them
   to follow helps build their confidence and comfort in interacting
   and engaging with people in all parts of the company.

5. Never define people by their job or title! What's inside a person
   defines who they are, not their job, so everyone should be treated
   with respect, worthy of your time as a leader. Create experiences
   that inspire, motivate, and develop a sense of ownership!

6. We should be open to feedback from others, but we must not
   empower others to determine our relevance.

Speak from Your Heart

1. An organization, which functions as a collective living being,
   sometimes needs the norm to be disrupted to make a point
   extremely clear and to establish focus. The key is to employ this
   mechanism rarely, lest it becomes the norm.

2. As a leader, you must consciously assess moments or situations
   as tools to affect a needed change, and use it to improve the
   organization.

3. There are a few areas of focus that leaders can employ to bring
   an organization together and focus on business goals. A strong
   emphasis on the health, safety, and well-being of everyone
   should be something everyone can understand and get behind.

4. Leaders in an organization must develop feedback skills, learning how to give focused counsel to employees.

5. The organization must hear from the leader's heart, not just their head.

Trust, But Verify

1. Every individual can get caught in a difficult situation by others. When that happens, it's important to listen intently to what is being said. But it's just as important to do some fact-finding of your own.

2. It's critical to follow up with those who ask questions or make claims, to let them know they are important to you.

3. Individuals who put themselves into awkward situations should be given the opportunity to learn from those moments and adjust their future actions accordingly. How many times you should offer such opportunities truly depends on the specific positive and negative contributions the individual delivers to the organization. If the negatives far outweigh the positives, fewer opportunities are warranted, and vice versa.

Inspirational Leadership Is Found at All Levels

1. It's the big things and the little things that communicate to others their value to you.

2. Preparation allows you to answer the knock of opportunity when it comes.

3. Sometimes, people make mistakes, but their effort and commitment are more valuable than the impact of their mistakes!

4. Hear what leaders say but listen to their actions.

5. Years later, a former Wake Forest football teammate shared with me that I was an inspiration to him — and he was a starter and team leader. I asked him why he made this comment and he said, "You brought everything you had to our team, you left it all on the field both in practice and in games, and you always came back for more, even when you shouldn't have because of your injured shoulder." The lesson: Even when you don't believe anyone is paying attention, they are!

Facing Adversity Reveals the Leader

1. Leaders are just people and they have stresses outside their professional roles. However, taking on a leadership role requires making the organization a high priority and being consistent.

2. Every member of the team, regardless of their position, is valuable as a person and deserves to be treated with respect (even the "walk-ons" in our lives!).

3. The true substance of a person is best seen when things go wrong, when pressure is at its height. These are situations when leaders go to what I've called their "root stock," when you get to see who they really are inside. Sooner or later, what sits in a leader's heart shows through, be it good or bad.

4. During times of stress and the worst of situations, organizations need challenges, but they also need re-enforcement and encouragement, with a large dose of "calm and collected."

5. Once the monster is out of the closet, it is nearly impossible to put it back. It's hard to forget the experience of seeing months of inspiration erased in a single 10-minute slice of time. Bad situations can be recoverable. However, they require humility

and slowly rebuilding with many positive experiences, as well as taking ownership of poor decisions and expressing sincere apologies in words and actions.

Opportunities in the Face of Uncertainty

1. To successfully operate a business, it is critical to invest time in defining expectations for leaders and employees at every level. View as an investment, not a cost, the importance of understanding the values of the organization, defining the competencies of leaders to lead by values, and the selection of the right individuals for the current and near-term business needs.

2. In the business world, personal relationships can override facts and data, especially when individuals involved are highly positioned.

3. Every experience can grow you and develop you, but it doesn't happen automatically. You mentally have to turn on this growth mindset, or you'll stunt your development and your career.

4. When you become so convinced about a path forward that requires other stakeholders to buy in, take time to evaluate the proposal from their point of view. You have to put your own thinking aside and evaluate the view of the other person — not how you *want* them to react, but how they likely *will* react.

5. Sometimes, you can derive learning and developmental benefits from the ultimate failure to achieve an objective, which will outweigh the disappointment over time.

Innovative Solutions with Clients

1. A mindset shift can change everything. For a team to accomplish a goal sometimes requires a different perspective, which can allow individuals and the group to overcome objections and fears, and to change their thinking. Strong leaders know when to remove themselves from the details of tasks to recognize the "big picture." Knowing how and when to do this is a critical instinct and skill to develop.

2. Innovation is a product of need to be fulfilled when there is no apparent solution.

3. Change, unplanned events, and external influences cannot always be controlled, but you have full control over how you respond.

4. The value of partnerships is enormous, specifically when you have a common goal and different views on how to accomplish the goal.

Build Two Resumes

1. Self-analysis of life priorities grounds us as individuals and helps us each truly see who we are as a person, beyond a role that we get paid to perform.

2. Life priorities evolve because life is not static. Keep updating, keep adding value, and keep challenging yourself to use your talents and capabilities to better your community, schools, and others in your life!

3. Other people in your life will benefit from your talents and skills, so share!

4. Prioritizing your life (vocations and avocations) ensures you invest your time to accomplish these priorities and fully engage yourself as a person.

ACKNOWLEGMENTS

There are so many people who have contributed to this book and my life, as my book and life are intertwined and inseparable. I will always be grateful and humbled by all the wonderful people whose life journeys have intersected with mine. I thank my Lord and Savior for the courage and thoughts He provided me in writing this book so I could share it with you.

When I began writing my book in earnest, writing quickly became a comfort to me during my business travels. As I completed the first draft, I enjoyed the process, but I didn't know whether my writing had merit. My wife and partner in life **Sandy**, my sons and best friends **Trey** and **Taylor**, my daughter-in-law **Annabel**, my mom and dad **Jerry** and **Teddy**, are not only inspirations to me, but they were early readers of my manuscript and encouraged me to pursue this project and launch this book. **Tim Doke**, Annabel's father, read and provided the first edits to my manuscript and encouraged me to "go for it," and then honored me by writing the foreword for the book. My family is precious to me, and I love them all dearly.

I want to specifically thank the wonderful leaders I've seen in my life, as they have provided examples that helped shape my beliefs and leadership style — **Jim, Walt, Rob, Anton, Laura, James, Syd, David, Bob** (who we recently lost), **Dan, Mel** and many others. I also want to acknowledge bosses who were not so positive, as I've learned from watching them as well.

I would be remiss if I did not acknowledge the thousands of people — colleagues and friends — who I've worked with in my career, played football with decades ago, and still keep in touch with through the years. My heart is full of appreciation for the support and guidance over the years, and the support and encouragement since my book's journey went public and they jumped on board to support me. The wonderful words of encouragement and endorsement from the dear people in my life that I've received have already made *Bosses Are Hired ... Leadership Is Earned* a success! Many of you immediately bought my book (even during the pre-order phase!) and your interest encouraged me further.

I'd like to thank the **Silver Tree Publishing** family. I'm grateful to two-time Silver Tree business-book author **Rob Campbell** for introducing me to Silver Tree in the beginning of this publishing journey and making me believe that, with the right partner, remarkable things were possible. From my first phone call with Silver Tree, I knew I was in good hands. Silver Tree founder and president **Kate Colbert** played so many roles in this project: encourager, marketer, leader of talent, and friend! Kate's skills as an editor have elevated my book to a different level, and I'm so grateful for her guidance and wisdom that she continued to share throughout the process. From the beginning, I knew Silver Tree was the partner for me! **Stephanie Feger** has been such a blessing in helping me traverse the world of marketing and promoting, social media, publicity, and branding. **Courtney Hudson's** cover design blew me away the first time I saw it, and I'm still inspired by her creativity, which transformed my book, inside and out. And **Penny Tate** kept me organized and informed every step of the way, always making me feel like her most important client.

One final acknowledgment to photographer **Rachel Ashcraft** for her wonderful talent in helping this old guy pose for the required pictures and head shots, to turn me from someone who wrote a book to an author who looked the part. The experience was outstanding and so are the results.

GO BEYOND
THE BOOK

Speaking/Inspiration

If you or your organization have an interest in a personal engagement with Carson, please contact him to speak to your class, team, or organization to share his insights with you.

Career Coaching

Every professional needs a coach they can trust to confidentially work through situations, career paths, and business and organizational challenges. And not every professional — especially those early in their careers and those at the top of their organizational charts — has an in-house mentor they can rely on. If you need a relationship with a coach who has no other motivation outside of helping you be the best you can be, please reach out to Carson@CarsonSublett.com or visit CarsonSublett.com to learn more!